S

Practical remedial measures, including ~~~~~~ ~ ~~
day diet, for the treatment of skin complaints.

SKIN TROUBLES

*Prepared and produced by the Editorial Committee
of Science of Life Books.*

Revised and Extended

SCIENCE OF LIFE BOOKS
11 Munro Street, Port Melbourne, Victoria 3207

Sixth edition, revised and reset, 1984
Second Impression 1986

Inquiries should be made to the publishers:
Lothian Publishing Company Pty. Ltd.
11 Munro Street, Port Melbourne, 3207

U.K. Distributors:
THORSONS PUBLISHING GROUP
Wellingborough, Northamptonshire
U.S.A. Distributors:
THORSONS PUBLISHERS INC.
Rochester, Vermont

National Library of Australia card number
and ISBN 0-909911-05-3

Printed and bound in Great Britain

Contents

Foreword

Skin problems are with us virtually from 'the cradle to the grave' and he is a very fortunate person indeed, who, at some time or another throughout life does not suffer from some form of skin disorder. In many cases skin troubles are short lived, or are of a transitory nature, such as sunburn, or an attack of hives after the sufferer has eaten something which disagrees with him or her. These minor problems are often passed off as unimportant and forgotten about. There are, however, a great many cases where skin problems are of a chronic nature, being very persistent and difficult to clear up, often persisting over a period of years and becoming alternatively better, then worse, or gradually deteriorating as age advances. For these unfortunate people there appears to be no real answer and many a person has become reconciled to live with the problem, obtaining from time to time what little relief the medical profession is able to offer when aggravation of the condition occurs.

Like so many other chronic conditions, the tendency towards skin problems can be inherited, and conditions such as asthma and eczema, or thyroid trouble and dry, scaly skin frequently run in families. It is not uncommon for a baby with infant eczema to be born into a family with a history of asthma. In the human embryo, the skin develops from the same basic cell as the nervous system, and it is not unusual for many nervous complaints to exhibit skin symptoms and for many skin problems to be made worse by nerve troubles.

The skin is one of the four major organs of elimination and is responsible together with the lungs, the kidneys and the large bowel for getting rid of toxins and waste matter from the body. If any of these other organs involved with elimination fail to function efficiently, then an increased load is placed on the eliminative capacity of the skin. As a result, some skin problems are nothing more than the body compensating for a shortcoming in the other organs of elimination. Where skin problems exist and there are kidney problems, respiratory trouble or constipation, the contribution these conditions may make to the problem should always be considered. For example, it is very difficult to clear up pimples, blackheads, etc., unless the diet is adjusted to prevent constipation. Constipation plays a significant role in many skin disorders.

Diet is also important, not only in providing adequate nutrition and supplying fibre for normal bowel function, but also in its influence on allergic reactions. To-day, allergies are becoming more and more important, particularly allergies to food additives such as artificial colourings, flavourings, preservatives, pesticide residues and other chemicals in foods.

Along with allergies to foods or food additives, there are allergies to soap, washing powders, detergents, bleaches and other household chemicals which can come into contact with the skin and cause an allergic reaction or a type of contact dermatitis. The importance of washing powders and detergents used to wash clothes or bed linen cannot be overlooked. These may not come into direct contact with the skin during the washing process. However residues left behind in clothes can be equally responsible for causing or aggravating skin troubles.

The skin also acts as a protective coating for the delicate structures beneath it. Nerves, blood vessels, muscles, tendons, etc., all rely on the skin for protection from outside influences. In severe conditions such as indolent ulcers, these subsurface tissues can be damaged.

Another function of the skin is to maintain normal body temperature using perspiration to cool the body in hot climates or during physical exertion, and helping to keep it warm in cold conditions. It can only do this effectively if it is kept healthy and in good order. Deep breathing can have a marked beneficial action on the skin not only by assisting to tone up other organs of elimination, but also in improving the circulation generally, the mental outlook and the overall condition of the central nervous system. When a skin condition appears, most people look for something 'to put onto it'; some external preparation to apply directly to the affected area. At best this usually only provides temporary relief and in most cases fails to remove the real cause of the problem. If the cause can be removed then the condition of the skin can return to normal.

There are a great number of factors which can contribute to skin problems. Sometimes these are obvious. However, more often they are obscure and difficult to recognize. The value of vitamins in the prevention and treatment of skin ailments has been known for many years and many people have benefited from the use of vitamins and other food supplements. In recent years our knowledge of minerals, trace elements and their value in nutrition has expanded rapidly. As a result, zinc has in many cases become an essential ingredient in the management of many skin problems. Zinc is a trace element which is vitally essential to the maintenance of normal functions of the skin and mucous membranes. The mucous membranes are an extension of the skin, lining the surfaces of the digestive tract, lungs, etc., inside the body. The mucous membrane is similar in structure to the skin and functions inside the body in much the same way as the skin does outside. Our 'Western style' diet is marginally deficient in zinc, providing only about 13mg per day as against a requirement of 15-20mg per day. Zinc is an important factor in promoting the healing of slow-healing wounds, ulcers (both internal and external), burns, etc. It also has a beneficial effect in the treatment of acne, particularly during adolescence where the zinc requirement can increase by up to 300%. Another significant property of zinc is in promoting normal keratinogenesis. Hyperkeratosis in elderly people often responds to zinc supplements.

One of the major uses of zinc is fast becoming its ability to assist in the treatment of cold sores (herpes). Zinc not only helps to speed up the healing process but also helps to assist in preventing the multiplication of the herpes virus. More recently another trace element, selenium, shows potential benefit in the treatment of psoriasis. In psoriasis, the body produces an excessive amount of substances called leukotriennes. Selenium has the capacity to inhibit the formation of leukotriennes and so exercise a beneficial effect both in the treatment and prevention of psoriasis. Considerable progress in our knowledge of skin disorders and measures to help the unfortunate sufferers has been made in recent years. As knowledge increases, it can only add to our understanding of the problem. This book is designed to give the reader a better understanding of his or her individual problem so that they will be in a better position to help themselves.

WILLIAM KING D.O., D.C.
New South Wales

1

What the Skin Is and Does

The skin is one of the most extraordinary mechanisms of the body. Says Dr Logan Clendening in *The Human Body:* 'It is that outer rampart which separates us from the rest of the universe. The sack that contains that juice, or essence which is me, or which is you; a defence against insects, poisons, germs and surgeons, through which they must break before they can storm the citadel. A great dermatologist has called the skin 'the mirror of the system'. How its texture and colour change with changes in bodily health — now white with pallor of fatigue or sepsis, now blue with the cyanosis of heart failure, now greyish yellow with what physicians call the cachexia of degenerative disease! It reacts to heat by pouring our perspiration, which cools on evaporation; to bitter cold, to the light of the sun, to the blowing of the winds. The very storms of the soul are recorded upon it — the deep flush of anger or humiliation, the pale tenseness of fear or excitement, the sparkling iridescence of triumph or of ecstacy. The end organs of feeling, attaching it, by a million fine nerve filaments to the brain, are largely responsible for our feeling of personality and entity.' This bulwark that stands between you and the world adds up to about 20 square feet in size, varying in thickness. On your eyelids, it is about $\frac{1}{25}$ of an inch thick. The thickest skin on your feet might be ¼ of an inch thick.

Your hide is much more than a protective overcoat. It has several vital functions. It keeps temperatures on an even keel; gives warning through its nerve 'sentries' of threats to the body, whether excess heat or cold, sharp objects, or changes in texture. The skin provides much of our information about the world around us, via its sensory powers, plus the amazingly astute sense of touch. The skin is one way that the body can rid itself of waste products of metabolism. It manufactures the pigment that screens us from sunlight, new nails and hair, and constantly replaces its surface with new cells. If its surface is damaged, it has astounding powers to restore itself as though nothing had ever happened.

Thermostat

The skin's most vital role is keeping the body at an even temperature. The vasomotor nerves have power to dilate or contract its blood vessels. The secretory nerves give orders to two million sweat glands. When the weather is warm, the blood vessels enlarge to let heat escape, and the sweat glands pour out as much as half a gallon of water a day to keep you comfortable. Even on a day when you are not aware of heat, your skin will dispose of about one pint of liquid. Because it will evaporate as soon as it reaches the surface, you won't be aware of sweating. But this liquid can both act as temperature control, and carry out with it some waste products.

In this way, the body can maintain virtually the same temperature, give or take a degree or two, while the world outside can be 10 degrees cooler or hotter. Without this system, changes in our body temperature of only a few degrees hotter or colder could halt vital body functions. If we run a temperature of even 37.8°C/100°F, for instance, only two degrees above normal, we're likely to feel ill. Three degrees more, and hospitals are likely to rush in the ice-packs. When cold attacks us, the skin reacts differently. First, it drives the blood from the surface of the skin further into the centre of the body, where it can be warmed again. Then the pores contract, and 'goose-flesh' forms to thicken the surface so that the cold cannot go through the skin so fast. Finally, the warmed blood is re-supplied to the surface. The skin-nerves telegraph, as it were, the need for continued supplies of warm blood to the heart and lungs, so as to maintain a defensive cordon of warmth. Hence the warm glow which follows a cool shower or walk in cold air, or a swim. If the cold is even more severe or long-lasting, the skin plays its last card: it shivers. Shivering is an involuntary muscular exercise, and like all other exercise, generates heat so that the cold cannot penetrate.

But if severe heat is the problem, the skin will flush with blood in order to let it get as near as possible to the surface so that it can cool off. The lungs are 'instructed' to produce only as much heat as bodily functions require. The heart is speeded up to make the blood circulate faster through the skin 'radiator'.

The lower amount of heat needed by the body in hot conditions means that people who live in the Tropics are estimated to have a 'basal metabolism', or basic calorie usage, some ten per cent lower than in temperate climates.

According to *Human Nutrition and Dietetics* (7th edition, Davidson, Passmore, Brock and Truswell), studies of a group of British and a group of Sudanese students, first in Cambridge during the winter and later in Khartoum during the summer, both places having similar programmes of work and leisure, showed that in Khartoum, a substantial reduction took place in both food intake and energy expenditure. It is suggested that where the mean annual temperature is over 25°C/77°F, five to ten per cent fewer calories need to be eaten. Much of this saving is due to the skin's conservation. However, modern central heating or air-conditioning does its best to minimize the skin's need to adapt to different temperatures. Skin hair is part of this temperature regulating system, with our head hair helping keep the head warm. Without such a covering, children in particular, may lose body heat quickly via the scalp. Hair may help body cooling by holding sweat as it evaporates on leaving the body. It may help keep us warm when necessary by bristling when we are cold, and in very hairy people, providing an approximation to a fur coat.

The insulating cushions of fat beneath the skin also help keep us warm. They tend to disappear in old age, which explains in part why Grandpa grumbles more about the cold. We also take for granted the wonderful waterproofing of the skin. Its overlapping, fishlike scales are punctured by millions of tiny holes — the pores. Yet because of its oil glands, which provide an undetectable layer of waterproofing oil, and its ingenious structure, you can stay under water for an indefinite time without having your organs waterlogged. The tiny oil glands — about two million — also keep the surface from being overdried by the air. It is the value of this layer, which keeps the skin soft and through its acid composition deters many bacteria from thriving on the skin surface or breaking through it, that makes soap so dubious a health or beauty aid. Soap simply washes away the natural protection — leaving the skin vulnerable to dryness, infection or itching. The exceptions are soaps specially altered in composition so that the usually alkaline nature of soap is matched to the acidity of the skin.

When a product states that it is 'pH-balanced', it means that the acid balance has been changed so that it is at a number close to the 6.5 to 7 that connotes 'neutral skin'. The lower the number, the more acid the product. Rain water may have acquired its reputation as a skin beautifier because it is naturally a little acid. As well as pH-balanced soaps, there are also 'wash bars' which are non-soap and pH-balanced, for those who don't feel clean without washing. Another option is to use a pH-balanced wash, following with a very dilute solution of cider vinegar (acid) in water, often recommended for the relief of an itchy skin.

Waste Disposal Unit

The skin supplements the bowels and kidney as a method of waste disposal. Skin elimination goes on all the time through the 'insensible perspiration' described earlier. A good sweat will help the body get rid of more waste products. So anti-perspirants or tight clothing can lead to the body retaining wastes that would otherwise have been easily disposed of.

Vitamin Catcher

Yet another function of the skin is to absorb sunlight which the body can use to make vitamin D, the vitamin that we need to make full use of the calcium we eat. The calcium is essential for the manufacture of bone as well as for nerve-muscle health.

Although some foods, especially oily fish, supply vitamin D, sunlight on the skin is the main and most important source. This is yet another benefit of exercise, since the heat produced by activity means that we are likely to uncover more skin to the sunlight than we might when still. Vitamin D can be stored by the body for some time. Children who have had a summer holiday will still have higher vitamin D levels the following winter than children who had no summer sun. It is considered (Loomis, 1967) that the pink cheeks of a European infant, with an area of about 20 square centimetres, can daily produce about 10 micrograms of vitamin D if exposed to open sunlight (i.e., not through glass). This is enough to prevent rickets, the bandy leg condition that used to be extremely common among children, who suffered weak bones that buckled under their weight as a result of poor calcium intake coupled with poor vitamin D supply so that the calcium they did eat was not well used by the body.

Another factor in the previous epidemic of rickets was that sunlight was blocked off from the skin by the pall of industrial smoke and pollution that hung over large industrial cities. This factor is waning, but sunlight on the skin is still essential. The sun does not have to be shining unimpeded by clouds — but won't work through glass. So when people talk about 'fresh air being good for you', they should be referring as much to the light on the skin as air in the lungs. As with most things, moderation is essential for the skin to benefit from sunlight. Too much direct strong sun will not only burn the skin. It can also dry it out excessively, encouraging wrinkles but also depressing its natural anti-infective powers. The more fair-skinned you are, the more cautious you need to be to limit the amount of sun on the skin to, say, under 40 minutes in fierce sun. You do not need to worry when the British sunlight, without fierce direct sun, is your environment. Forty minutes of exposure in strong sun is ample for helping skin complaints or forming vitamin D.

Your skin is a good mirror of your general health. For it is not just a covering bag that keeps us in one piece, but an important organ of the body. Most of the many skin troubles for which people consult their doctors are not just skin troubles. They are symptoms that this organ (and other organs of the body) are being affected by some more general bodily disturbance. That is the case even if no other obvious symptoms are present. How the skin looks is an important indicator to a practitioner of what may be wrong: its colour, for instance, can indicate liver problems, angina, poor circulation, anaemia or emotional strain. Once you realize this, then you stop seeing skin problems as something to be tackled only externally, by lotions or ointments. These may relieve discomfort, but they won't usually cure the problem permanently, for its cause will still be there. That may be something with a name, known to bring with it skin symptoms — such as measles, shingles or jaundice. In these cases, practitioners recognize that the skin problem will right itself when the underlying illness goes away.

In other cases, the underlying condition is not understood. Then the skin disease gets a name of its own, such as acne, dermatitis or boils, and is treated in most cases as though only the skin were affected. This is misleading, if it tempts people to regard their skin complaint as a disease in itself. For such complaints are most successfully tackled by searching for an underlying cause in your style of life. What you eat, your job, and how you react to the problems of everyday life may all be contributing to what you may see as a skin problem that has happened to arrive on you.

Tackling such underlying causes is the way to cure your skin condition permanently — with the benefit that at the same time you will be improving your general health, since other functions will almost certainly be suffering as well as your skin, even if they do not show it so obviously. Most drugs given to treat skin problems do not attempt to get at the underlying causes: they aim to relieve symptoms. This in itself makes them an unsatisfactory form of treatment, and their side-effects can be substantial. Since they rarely solve the problem permanently, the taker is faced with possible recurrence, or taking the drugs and undergoing side-effects over a long period, while the underlying disturbance may go untreated.

This book is about the non-drug methods of treating

skin problems by correcting the habits or circumstances to which the body is reacting badly. Such methods call for more effort than swallowing medicines or applying creams. Our habits of life can be hard to alter. However, the benefits of this effort can be a beacon to work towards. Firstly, the natural treatments are safe — with no short-term unpleasant effects, and no long-term fear about safety. Secondly, natural treatments, which aim to tackle the cause and not only the symptoms, hold the promise of permanent relief. Thirdly, they will usually be helping your general health too, and many minor ailments never consciously connected with your skin problem may also right themselves. Feeling generally well, with energy and interest in life, doesn't just feel good. It also promotes mental well-being — which in turn can help your job, your family life and your relationships.

Skin Facts and Fallacies

1. 'Acne is perfectly normal at your age. There is no use in doing anything about it, as it will probably go away by the time you are older.' Fallacy. Acne can permanently scar a young person, physically as well as psychologically. And natural treatment can relieve it without resorting to drugs.

2. 'The older I get, the more I seem to itch. Although I bathe more often, the itch is not relieved.' Fact. As people age, the sebaceous glands which provide oil for the skin, become less active. But washing with soap just makes the condition worse, by washing off what natural oil is produced, leaving the skin dry and irritable. Use water alone, with soap only once a week, if your skin is itchy. Choose an acid (pH)-balanced wash bar, and follow with oil on the skin.

3. 'This dandruff remover is guaranteed to clear my scalp.' Fallacy. No dandruff remover can possibly cure dandruff — see under Dandruff for reasons. Such shampoos and treatments may alleviate the condition, but they aren't curing it.

4. 'Soap is a good antiseptic, so I'll scrub my spots and rashes with it — and it will help dry them up.' Fallacy. Soap is not particularly good for a healthy skin, let alone a sick one. Use water instead, as soap will wash off natural protection, and can hinder the healing process.

5. 'This may be a skin cancer, but I'll just watch it for a time and see what happens.' Fallacy. There is nothing to be gained by 'watching' any suspected malignancy. If you have the slightest suspicion that the spot on the skin may be cancerous, lose no time in having it medically checked.

2

The Basic Scene

Most skin complaints do not have a single cause, but are the product of a combination of circumstances. Although the symptoms of your particular form of skin condition may be quite different from those of another sufferer, some of the same conditions are likely to underlie both problems.

1. Heredity: A tendency to certain skin problems can be inherited — so that if the circumstances are right (or rather, wrong) you are more likely to show your body's dissatisfaction in the way your parents did than is someone whose parents either had no skin problems, or had different forms of them. Among the inherited tendencies are those to dermatitis, eczema, psoriasis, and acne. However, the fact that you have a tendency to a particular complaint does not mean that it is inevitable. Instead of making you resign yourself to suffer, this knowledge might strengthen your resolve to do everything you can to reduce your vulnerability. For one thing, part of the inherited tendency may have nothing to do with your genes, and everything to do with inherited patterns of living — such as the style of meals your family favours, their exercise habits and so on.

Since prevention is usually much easier than cure, any one who knows that skin problems exist in their family is sensible to check that their own way of life is not inviting the same problems. If you suffered eczema as a child, for instance, read the section on eczema and you'll find some very avoidable causes — such as taking cow's milk too early — which affect some children. Then you can dodge this possible (although far from certain) problem with them. Your family's experience may also tip you off as to the best way to tackle a skin problem. If someone closely related to you by blood has found a particular treatment effective, it's more likely that you will find it helpful too. And they may have tried and rejected other treatments — which you might then decide to put low down on your list of possibilities. Family tendencies are significant, but should be used to alert yourself to preventitive measures, rather than as a reason to resign yourself.

2. *What you eat:* We will talk about how poor eating habits can encourage your system to react to everyday stress in a 'strained' way, see page 24. That's one consequence of poor nutrition which can help set the scene for skin problems. Another is more direct. Here are some of the ways in which the food you eat can make skin problems worse:

a. Food intolerance — see page 31.
b. Failure to supply the body with all the raw materials it needs to maintain health. The skin won't be the only part of the body affected, but it may show it most obviously. About 40 nutrients have so far been found to be essential to human health. These include:

● Vitamins — at least 14 are recognized as essential, and more if you could their different forms. Vitamin E, for instance, is a 'family name' covering four related substances.

● Minerals — about 20 are known to be required. These can be grouped into minerals of which the body needs substantial amounts, and 'trace elements' — of which only a trace is needed. However, shortage of a trace element can produce just as bad effects as deficiency of a major-quantity mineral.

- Proteins — about eight of the protein 'family' of amino acids are described as 'essential' in the sense that the body cannot make these, as it can some 12 other proteins, from other substances in food. The essential amino acids can only be obtained from food.

- Fats — are something most of us eat too much of, but some may still fail to eat enough of the kinds of fat that supply what are called 'essential fatty acids' — again, available to the body only by food, not by its own manufacturing abilities. The essential fatty acids are considered to be linoleic acid, and linolenic acid. They are mainly found in ultra-soft fats, for example, oils. When an oil or fat claims to be 'high in poly-unsaturated fatty acids', it will contain more of these essential fatty acids, or EFA's. In oils, linseed, safflower, sunflower and soya oil are the richest in polyunsaturates. Soft margarine, *provided* it is labelled 'high in polyunsaturates', and the oil contained in oily fish are the best other sources.

- Carbohydrates — including the indigestible carbo-hydrates known as dietary fibre, are an important part of the food we eat. To call them 'just stodge' conceals their importance as the food that avoids the problems of too much fat, too much sugar or too little fibre. Plant foods are also the essential source of vitamin C, as well as offering a range of other vitamins, mainly B group and E, and of minerals and trace elements. These virtues of carbohydrate do not apply to the 'simple sugar' type of carbohydrate, sucrose or ordinary white sugar. It provides nothing but calories, which while a necessary item, should 'pay their way' by carrying with them some of the other nutrients we need. Sugar carries nothing with it that will help your health.

A shortage in any of the raw materials which your body uses to function normally will lead to a health problem sooner or later. This may well produce skin symptoms. On page 63, you'll find a simple set of guidelines for making sure that you are not making your skin problem worse with every meal.

3. Exercise habits: Just like our other body organs, the skin is designed for an active life — the kind everyone used to have. If you don't give it some exercise, it will suffer. Poor circulation is a main result of too little exercise, and most people realize how much a good walk or a holiday spent in open air life can improve their skin's condition and tone. Yet people rarely think of exercise as one part of the natural way to tackle a skin problem. See chapter on exercise and diet, page 24.

3

Does Stress Cause Skin Disease?

Some people blame their skin problems on external stress. In fact, that is almost a contradiction in terms. Most stress depends on internal factors. Given the same set of circumstances, Mr A is likely to react differently from Mr B — showing that most external *stresses* only become a *strain* if our individual reaction to them is poor. Some people can tolerate a great deal of difficulty in life — others find what seems a calm and pleasant existence a great strain.

What *is* true is that a situation you find a strain is likely to worsen almost any condition you suffer from, including a skin condition. So strain can be a trigger, rather than a direct cause. And there are natural methods (not tranquillizers) of improving one's tolerance of stress — to which everyone, after all, is exposed every day. Three main aids to stopping stress becoming strain are eating healthily, exercise and mental attitudes.

Food: How can food help? Eating healthily helps you feel well — and that in turn encourages cheerfulness. Physical as well as mental resilience can be 'fed' by the right food, so that you cope better with life. Some foods we often use actively encourage stress. Too much alcohol saps our sense of being able to cope, and in control — as well as being a depressant after the first 'high'. Too much caffeine or its related stimulants, mainly in coffee but also to some extent in tea, cola drinks and chocolate, also produces a stimulating period, which is inevitably followed by an anticlimax. In both cases, when the effects of alcohol and caffeine wear off, the temptation is to start the cycle again — leading to their use as a 'prop' instead of coming to terms with whatever is upsetting us.

When people are feeling under strain, they often lose interest in food, cooking and shopping. This may lead to subsisting on foods that are ready to eat and need no thinking about. Although this doesn't have to be an unhealthy way to eat, if you choose to subsist on, for instance, wholemeal bread, with cheese and cress, it can mean getting into the habit of living on biscuits, pies, crisps, buns, etc. These and many 'instant' foods are too high in sugar and in fat to form a balanced diet: too many calories are easily eaten, but because neither sugar nor fat provide many of the nutrients the body needs, you still don't get enough vitamins, minerals, fibre or, occasionally, protein. Under strain, many people gain weight rapidly, yet are worse supplied with the nutrients needed to maintain good health and resistance to infection. The result: lowered resistance to strain too. Other people lose interest in food so dramatically that they lose weight, and also go even shorter on vitamins, minerals and fibre.

For both groups, looks suffer as well as figure — adding to a strained situation the stress of feeling unwell and unattractive, and consequent loss of confidence. When people recognize they are under stress, a first move should be to improve the quality of what is eaten by increasing the intake of fruit, vegetables and unrefined cereals, at the expense of sugar, fat and over-refined foods which have lose nutrients in processing.

What should you eat? The guidelines on page 63 will provide basic materials for health. If you are under heavy stress, extra vitamin C is called for — as this vitamin is used more quickly then. A 500 milligram tablet or capsule each day is enough. If you smoke, you are adding more stress to your body's load, and using more vitamin C in all likelihood. Some estimates suggest that each cigarette calls for another 20-30 milligrams of vitamin C to be eaten, or roughly the amount in an orange. Since improving what you eat is often part of the natural treatment for skin complaints, you can do two favours to yourself at once: your meals to help skin directly may also help it indirectly by increasing your ability to cope with the stress that could be contributing to your skin problem.

Finally on food, the skin is one of the body's main routes for eliminating waste products. Ensure that those wastes are from healthy meals, and they are likely to be easier for the body to get rid of without too much effort.

Exercise: The mood-raising abilities of exercise are recognized by most people instinctively, even though they have only recently been explored scientifically. Most people have experienced how going for a good walk can lift them from a pessimistic mood, or how a wholehearted session of digging the garden can get an angry temper out of their system.

Almost all kinds of exercise seem to be valuable in helping people cope with stress, in a variety of ways:

● Providing an outlet for the 'ready for action' chemicals that the body produces when you are angry or afraid — the so-called 'fight or flight' response. If the body's preparation for crisis action is never followed by action, the stress chemicals — which are desirable during a crisis — may persist, and a situation of tension and tightness sets in.

● Exercise can absorb all your concentration, so

diverting you from any thought of your problems for a while. As well as providing a simple rest from them, such a break may put your problems into perspective, so they seem less daunting.

- Exercises that tend to make you breathless can lead to the production of brain chemicals which are natural antidepressants. These are known as catecholamines — including adrenaline and noradrenaline.

- All forms of exercise help you gain confidence in your own physical abilities. This enhances your general sense of being able to cope with life actively.

- Exercise helps use up energy, so you maintain your correct weight without restricting what you eat. Provided the foods you choose are ones which provide good supplies of vitamins, minerals, fibre and other nutrients as well as the calories which will be available as energy, you will end up being better nourished, simply because you are eating more. So you are likely to feel better — and perform better in life.

- All kinds of exercise improve your shape, and so your self-esteem — an important factor in resisting strain.

As with healthy eating, exercise has both direct and indirect benefits for your skin. In the points above, you'll see how it can help avoid stress affecting your skin. Then it can act directly by improving your circulation. The blood supply to the skin, which carries nutrients to cells, is a crucial part of having healthy skin. Without a good supply of nutrients, for instance, the skin becomes thin. The small blood vessels may break more easily, leading both to unsightly broken veins and possibly to inflamed skin. In old people, thin skin can heal poorly when broken, making them vulnerable to skin ulcers which last for months. Varicose veins are also encouraged, together with chilblains, loss of skin elasticity resulting in wrinkling, as well as general problems such as blockage of waste elimination.

Mental attitudes: The way that you tackle life can be the major factor in how stressful you find it, and so in skin problems if they are worsened by stress. Although it is part of the human condition to be by turns happier or unhappier, some people adopt attitudes to life which ensure that their ration of unhappiness will be considerable. Anyone who has fixed and lofty expectations of how life should turn out for them — in terms of relationships, career or finance — is practically guaranteeing themselves extra stress. For 'life' has not approved or even noticed their detailed blueprint, and is 100 per cent certain not to match it.

Stress has been defined as 'the gap between life as it is and life as we would like it to be'. The more rigid our idea of how it should be, the more often we are likely to get upset because it isn't like that. People who, while hoping and striving for the life they want, are prepared to adapt to how things turn out, are reducing their chances of getting upset all the time. When someone says something that upsets you, it is not compulsory that you get upset — it is usually because you think they should behave differently towards you. You have the choice of ditching your 'blueprint' of how you consider they should be, and so reacting to them simply as you find them. You can still get upset that way, but at least you are not ensuring that you do. Even if you still find their behaviour unsatisfactory, do you have to get upset about it? No — and the best way of convincing yourself of this is to reflect that there are almost certainly other people who would not get upset if they were at the receiving end of the behaviour in question. So why choose to get upset? Naturally, this does not apply to some situations, which would upset virtually anyone

— such as accidents, violence or loss of someone you love. When you do choose to get upset, it is certainly better for your health to let yourself express it. The 'stiff upper lip' is rather like suppressing the fight-or-flight response chemicals. The tension and emotion is left to fester, instead of being expressed and thereby dissipated.

A long way from skin health? Not at all. Ask many a skin sufferer, and they will confirm that when things are going well with their general life, their skin improves (even if their eczema or psoriasis does not disappear entirely). When life is not going their way, their skin gets worse again. Sometimes an emotional time does not cause a relapse, but a few days later, trouble starts. It's as though the body has held off, the better to concentrate on coping with the crisis, but then gives in under the strain when the situation relaxes a little.

4

Diseases of the Skin: External Causes and Remedies

Let's start with the exceptions: the skin troubles that are just skin troubles, and the result of an external cause.

Contact Dermatitis

About one in twenty people suffers skin reactions when they touch certain materials. Some materials cause reactions in most people. Some are quite harmless to most people, but set off strong and adverse reactions in a few. Typical symptoms are rashes, red patches, dry or scaly patches of skin, itching or little blisters. Detective work is often necessary to discover what is causing the reaction. The temptation is to suspect a new shampoo, or something that has touched your leg if the rash is on your leg. However, it isn't always so simple. Although it is true that the part of the body that has touched the guilty material is the part most often affected, other parts of the body may react as well, or instead of, that part — confusing you. The reaction may set in some time after the contact, making it difficult to connect the two. And although something new to you, like a new shampoo, is a common culprit, it's possible to become sensitive to something you've been touching without harm for years.

The obvious treatment is to keep away from the material that causes the trouble — especially since people usually stay over-sensitive to a substance. Cosmetics, houseplants, garden chemicals, pets, metals and fabrics are all suspect. Avoidance can be difficult if a material involved in your job is the culprit. But half measures don't usually help. Only small amounts of the material are necessary to set off the bad reaction, so total avoidance is called for. Doctors and your own detective work can help both identify suspect substances and test them to make sure you've found exactly what is causing the trouble. So contact dermatitis is a 'simple' skin problem. But if you are looking for culprits, don't forget that the substance does not have to touch the outside of your skin. Substances that you swallow, sniff or inhale can be the problem too.

Food Intolerance

Food intolerance is a better name than food allergy for skin problems provoked by particular foods. Not all food-related reactions are allergies in the strict sense of that word. If it is a food that you rarely eat that results in vomiting, swollen mouth, hives or skin rashes, it is not hard to track it down. A skin rash is not the only sign — headaches, bloated stomach, diarrhoea or a racing pulse may tell you that something is wrong first. But the cause of such discomfort is much more difficult to identify when it is an everyday food.

Dr James Lambert Mount, who treats many skin problems without resorting to drugs, speaks for many practitioners who treat food intolerance when he says that the most common causes are foods eaten so often that we don't suspect them. Coffee, tea, milk products and wheat come top of his list of foods that people cannot tolerate. He does not believe that these bad reactions are 'born into' the sufferers. He blames them instead on taking in too much of the substance, in a poor quality form, for too long. He doesn't blame the many cases of eczema he treats, for instance, on milk itself — but on the *kind* of milk most people drink, and in large amounts every day. It is the processing of milk, including cooking it for pasteurization, and the residues of medicines given the cows as a result of intensive farming practice, that he thinks have turned it and its products into 'problem foods' for many people. When Dr Richard Mackarness investigated food intolerance in his book *Not All In The Mind*, he was more concerned with the effects of foods on people's mental health. But skin symptoms were a common by-product.

Since the commonness of such intolerances has been recognized, methods of identifying the 'problem foods' have been worked out. The most used are 'elimination diets'. Here, the sufferer spends five to seven days eating only two or three foods which are seldom the cause of bad reactions, and drinking only bottled spring water. The common foods chosen are either a combination of lamb and pears; or cod and peas. During this regime, the sufferer from symptoms thought to be due to intolerance of certain food or foods should notice a definite improvement. If the skin has been suffering, it should get better quite quickly. After five to seven days, the sufferer eats some of a food particularly suspected of causing a bad reaction. Some doctors don't like the patient to swallow the food, as if it is the culprit, its sudden reappearance may cause a strong adverse reaction. Instead, they prefer to put a little under the tongue and wait to see the reaction. If the person is intolerant to the food, some reaction can be expected within hours and sometimes within minutes. Some specialists particularly look out for a quickening of the pulse as a sign of food intolerance. As well as looking out for this after an elimination diet, they suggest that people can pulse test themselves while eating normally. Any food after which the pulse speeds up markedly is suspect. After an elimination diet, only one food is added back to meals each day, and hopefully, one or more foods which cause a reaction will be identified.

This appears, and is, a potentially tedious process, especially if you don't guess successfully and therefore try first the foods which you might react badly to: specialists would follow Dr Mount's four by chocolate, eggs and then your favourite foods. If you do track down the culprit(s), you have a choice of avoiding the food entirely, or asking a homoeopath whether it might be possible to desensitize you using a minute amount of a remedy that in large amounts would produce similar symptoms to those you are suffering. What if you seem to have allergic reactions to many everyday foods on which your meals largely depend? This is when you might stop seeing a food intolerance as a piece of luck, bad but unavoidable, to which the only response is avoidance of the foods.

If you turn out to be a super-sensitive person, it begins to beg the question 'why?', especially if you have not always been. In cases like these, the intolerance seems only part of a wider breakdown of the body's ability to cope. A programme to build up general health, under the care of a qualified practitioner, using food, exercise and stress control, is justified. Otherwise, the same 'poor coping' which stops the body coping with food well, could also be reducing its ability to deal with other parts of your life, including the viruses and bacteria which surround us all but are normally well resisted by body defence systems. Some help in identifying food intolerances is available under the National Health Service, although not as much as with contact dermatitis. For food, you may have to hunt harder for professional help, especially if you want to overcome a general over-sensitivity. Unfortunately, some 'experts' believe they can track down food allergies by near-psychic means, for instance, by you sending them a lock of your hair, a spot of your blood, etc. Other practitioners are apt to blame every ailment on food intolerance, and put people on rigid diets which cut them off from social or family life for no proven benefit. Be wary of allergy specialists who do not belong to a professional association which stipulates a non-postal, thorough training in their speciality. See page 76 for guidance on finding a practitioner.

Impetigo

This infectious skin complaint is far rarer, thanks to improvements in housing and hygiene. Most common among children, it takes the form of pustules with thick surface crusts. Once again, infection is more likely where resistance has been lowered by poor eating habits — and improving eating habits can help the body recover quickly. Children under seven years old can be given one vitamin A capsule, one vitamin B complex supplement and 100mg of vitamin C daily. Older children can have twice the amount of vitamin B and C, but don't double the vitamin A. Don't use soap on the area. However, washing with a mixture of a few tablespoons of cider vinegar to a small cup of water can act as a cleansing antiseptic.

Psoriasis

One of the most difficult skin conditions to treat either by natural or by drug methods, psoriasis appears as red patches which are covered with thin, dry, silvery-coloured scales. As the scales fall off, new ones form, but in some cases, the area will become raw and sore. The areas most often affected are the elbows, knees and scalp, although it can also affect the trunk. Dr D. Roe, dermatologist and nutrition scientist at Cornell University, U.S.A. pointed out that the incessant scaling of the skin, with the formation of new scales, causes extraordinary losses of vitamins and minerals even in those who eat enough of these for normal needs. Psoriasis is frequently associated with arthritis, and it is possible that it is these losses which adversely affect the bony structure of the body, and encourage the development of arthritis.

According to Dr Roe, studies made by the Clinical Nutrition Unit of Cornell University disclose that psoriasis is due to a metabolic incapacity to use the protein, taurine. This amino acid occurs in bile combined with bile acids. As well as being supplied by food, taurine is made within the body. But it may be that psoriasis sufferers are unable to cope with it because of an enzyme deficiency. The researchers thought that psoriasis sufferers might benefit by cooking the taurine out of foods like meat. If meat is boiled for five minutes (after which it can be cooked further by another method) most of the taurine is eliminated. The initial boiling water should be thrown away. For other people, this method is not recommended, as some of the B vitamins in the food will also be dissolved out.

Natural treatments

Food: For a general healthy diet, see page 66. Any nutrient losses which may have been caused by psoriasis should be made good by taking supplements. A reasonable mixture would include:

Lecithin: According to the *New York Journal of Medicine* (1950), the psoriatic skin contains about over three times more cholesterol than normal skin. The *Journal* continues: 'Of 155 patients treated with lecithin, 118 (76%) were controlled or improved.' The treatment took from one to five months, depending on the severity of the case. After that, a lower amount of lecithin maintained the improvement. A German skin specialist, Dr Sigwald Bommer, says that the blood of those with psoriasis has much less lecithin in it than that of non-sufferers. He advises that lecithin be taken daily. Granules extracted from soya beans, eggs or sunflower seeds are easy to buy. They provide some essential fatty acids as well as B vitamins choline and inositol. Lecithin is also a natural emulsifier (a property for which it is used in many foods). This ability to break fat into small globules that will stay suspended in watery liquids may also play a part in its effect.

The *International Medical Digest* of April 30, 1965 detailed the successful treatment of psoriasis by Russian scientists, using vitamin C, vitamin B_{12} and the B vitamin folic acid. In Britain, folic acid is not sold as a supplement, but is usually included in the formulae of multi-vitamin supplements. Extra minerals are also worthwhile, such as a multi-mineral chelated supplement. Another way of boosting mineral intake is by taking up to ten kelp tablets a day.

Naturopath Leon Chaitow recommends generous amounts of extra vitamins for treating 'this stubborn condition': 800IU of natural vitamin E per day, 15,000 to 25,000 of vitamin A, 30 to 60mg of vitamin B_6 (pyridoxine) and eight to ten brewer's yeast tablets, to provide extra B vitamins and minerals. Exposure to sunlight is often helpful, or even sunlamps. But it's most effective when combined with sea bathing.

Other treatments

The stubbornness of psoriasis makes it worth considering a visit to a health farm of the sort that uses nature cure to start the healing process. This makes possible a supervised fast, which often helps start the process. Sufferers who follow this advice in diet and supplements may be alarmed to find that their symptoms at first seem to worsen. This does often happen as the body mobilizes its defences to restore health. It's necessary to accept this period as a sign of better times to come. This so-called 'healing crisis' occurs with many ailments when naturally treated. The best way to cope with it is to let it make you more confident that this treatment is correct.

Some of the drugs given to relieve psoriasis are extremely likely to have unpleasant side-effects, especially as the sufferer is likely to be told that they must be taken more or less permanently. Safer are coal tar ointments and shampoos. A homoeopath may also be helpful. Washing the skin with soap or anti-acne treatments in an effort to clear it will be worse than useless: you will only irritate the skin and stimulate even more shedding and production of skin cells. Itching will also be worsened by 'cleansing' local treatments, anti-dandruff shampoos or soap.

The treatment known as PUVA has a natural base. This is the abbreviation for Psoralens-Ultra-Violet-light-A. Psoralens are substances that increase the skin's sensitivity to sunlight. The best known natural source is bergamot oil, used to flavour Earl Grey tea as well as in assorted tanning preparations (eg. the *Bergasol* range). While their role in tanning aids is considered controversial, in that increasing the skin's sensitivity to sunlight might also reduce its protection against skin cancer, the substance may be useful for psoriasis sufferers. The medical treatment used is to take a psoralen by mouth and then ultra violet light of the particular wavelengths known as A. The psoralen apparently binds with DNA, part of the genetic cell reproduction system, and this interferes with the abnormally rapid production of cells of which psoriasis consists. The treatment also causes increased production of melanin, the tanning and browning pigment, in the exposed areas, and can produce skin inflammation. This reaction may explain why psoriasis sufferers tend to improve in sunshine. The medical form of the treatment has been evaluated as clearing about 85 per cent of patients of virtually all, or all, of their psoriatic patches. However, the effect is not permanent, and 'top-up' treatments may be needed within one to six months.

Shingles

The *herpes zoster* virus produces blistering eruptions and nerve pain that can be intense. It can vary from a moderate burning sensation, to very severe pain on the left side of the chest, which gives some people the impression that their heart is affected. The blisters always affect one side, perhaps on the back, or forming a half girdle round the side of the body to the middle of the chest, but also often on the face near the eyes or mouth, or the groin. The virus is closely related to the one that causes chicken pox. The virus runs its course in from two to four weeks, and there is little that can be done to shorten that course. As well as pain, sufferers often feel feverish and very depressed.

Shingles occurs mostly in people over 50, and more often in men. The virus is infectious, but the fact that you contract it is generally a sign of poor resistance. When the blisters eventually dry up, they look a little like overlapping tiles — hence the name of shingles. One attack gives immunity to further attacks, but sometimes there remains neuralgic, or nerve, pain, which if not tackled can last for months.

Natural treatments

Relieving the pain is the first problem. Acupuncture may well be ideally suited to this problem. Homoeopaths recommend Rhus. Tox. and Natrum Mur. 30, both taking two tablets every two hours until symptoms subside. Tepid baths, of about blood heat, using a seaweed bath extract can help.

Food: The obvious aim is to build resistance as fast as

possible. As well as following a high quality diet, (see page 63), extra vitamin A, C and B group are recommended, as suggested for psoriasis.

Herbs: Oats is the herbal specific for nerve problems, and can be taken as a decoction as well as in the form of porridge, muesli or oatcakes. Damiana and pain-killing herbs such as meadowsweet may be useful.

Supplements: A vitamin particularly connected with relieving shingles is vitamin B_{12}. This is often available to sufferers from their doctors in the form of injections, which allow larger quantities to be absorbed.

Many shingles sufferers have a history of taking aspirin or other drugs over long periods. This may contribute to their eventual vulnerability to the virus, if the drugs have resulted in a lowering of their resistance. Similar lack of resistance may be linked with a previous illness of long duration, long-established poor eating habits, or a prolonged period of stress or overwork.

Tinea (athlete's foot)

Tinea is a fungus disease. It's infectious, but needs the right environment to thrive. That environment includes a warm, moist atmosphere around the skin of the toes. The result is raw, eroded skin, with both itching and burning pain if the rawness worsens. Athlete's foot is a good name for it, because the sweating and extra heat caused by exertion, coupled with frequent showers from the floor of which the fungus can be caught, and topped off by lack of care in drying between the toes, provide an ideal recipe for encouraging tinea. Summer is the worst time for tinea.

To discourage the problem, wear the best-ventilated socks and footwear available, preferably in natural

materials. Whenever possible, wear sandals or open shoes
without socks, or go barefoot. Wash between the toes often,
with plain water or a weak solution of permanganate of
potash. You can also add a little cider vinegar to the
washing water. Then dry thoroughly between the toes.
This is most easily done by air drying using a hair dryer
or fan heater, set to the coolest temperature. You can also
wind a strip of cotton wool in and out of your toes, to keep
them apart so that the air can get in. A special drying 'paint'
can be bought at chemists, to put on after washing. At
places where the infection is rife, such as swimming pools,
use their disinfectant foot bath, and if you find you easily
get athlete's foot, wear the specially designed 'footlets' sold
for swimming.

Urticaria

Also known as hives or nettle rash, urticaria is usually an
allergic reaction, taking the form of a rash with itching.
Urticaria is a common side-effect of many drugs, including
medicinal ones, as well as of some food allergies. Although
urticaria is a minor problem, it should not be ignored, since
other side-effects from the same cause can be much more
serious although invisible. An example of a substance that
is commonly used, and which can cause urticaria is
tartrazine, an azo dye, which is used to colour many foods
and drinks. Orange, red and green foods are the most likely
to contain it. The same colouring has also been connected
to asthma (Zlotlow and Settipane, 1977).

There is no external way of clearing up the conditions:
you have to remove the cause. No medicine will do this
either. If rashes persist for no apparent reason, start looking
for some substance, including a food, to which the sufferer
might be allergic. Once again, soap washes will not help
the situation, and may well make a rash or itch worse.
Instead, use cold water compresses, and soothing infusions

such as marigold (calendula) or aloe vera.

Vitiligo

Also known as leukoderma, vitiligo is a painless skin condition which produces loss of pigment on patches of skin. The patches can be any shape or size. Vitiligo is thought to be due to failure by the body to produce melanin, the brown pigment that produces freckles or suntan. Why this failure should affect patches, and why it suddenly occurs, is not understood. However, known causes can be pregnancy — especially if a woman has a lot of bright sunshine on the skin during or just afterwards; wounds where the scars never recover the colour of surrounding skin; and burns. There is still no accepted cure. However, the B vitamin para-amino-benzoic acid, known as PABA, may be useful.

In an article written in the *Virginia Medical Monthly* in 1945 by Dr B. Sieve, teaching at Tufts' Medical School, this treatment is detailed. Dr Sieve treated a group of 25 women and 23 men, ranging in age from ten to 70. Some had had vitiligo for up to 28 years, others for only two years. After his treatment, some patients started to show improvement after four weeks, while others needed from eight to ten weeks. After six to seven months, the progress of all 48 patients was described as 'striking'. Dr Sieve considered that dietary deficiencies play an important part in causing vitiligo. The following remedial measures are suggested:

1. Eat well — following the basic plan on page 63.
2. Take 500mg of PABA a day. In the UK, this is not available in such large doses, so it's necessary to take more tablets or capsules.
3. Take one desiccated liver tablet three times a day.
4. Take one glutamic acid hydrochloride tablet three

times a day (available at health food stores or from Cantassium, 225 Putney Bridge Road, London SW15 2PY, tel. 01-870 0971).

5. Take a dessertspoonful of brewer's yeast in a glass of water, into which is stirred a dessertspoonful of skimmed milk powder. Sweeten if desired with a little honey or fruit purée.

The only other treatment so far explored for vitiligo is to take a psoralen, one of the substances that increases the body's sensitivity to sunlight, and its production of melanin. Natural psoralens from plants have apparently been used in India for this purpose. The best known natural psoralen here is oil from the bergamot fruit.

Bergamot is a herb that grows easily in Britain, its oil being used to flavour Earl Grey tea, and in tanning preparations. There has been suspicion that its use in suntan aids might sensitize the skin too much, increasing the risk of skin cancer. However, a survey of Sicilian workers involved in the extraction of bergamot oil from the fruit has not shown an increased rate of skin cancer so far, although further study is needed to exclude this possibility. A combination of bergamot and sunlight (turned into a medical treatment for psoriasis, see that section) might help vitiligo patches if the oil or sun tan aid is applied to the patch. However, this is not an established treatment.

Other Kinds of Allergies

Some other external causes of skin reactions, which the sufferer may not realize are producing these ill-effects are:

● Allergies to pollen, house mites, and dust.
● Smoke, your own or other people's, especially suspect if you also suffer from catarrh, sinus problems, asthma or wheeziness.

● Medicines. We quote from *The Skin Diseases* by Dr James Marshall, MD, BS, MRCS, LRCP, 'The number of drugs which can produce skin eruptions is enormous, and grows daily as new therapeutic substances come into use. The variety of eruptions is widely varied and almost any skin disease may be simulated.

Eruptions may be produced after ingestion of drugs, after intravenous or intramuscular injection, or after absorption through the skin or mucous membranes. Drug eruptions are seldom due to poisoning or toxicity; the determining factor is an individual cutaneous hypersensitivity to a particular substance or group of substances. Thus one man will produce an eruption after taking a certain drug, although others on exactly the same treatment have no reaction at all.' Dr Marshall then lists the following drugs as causes of certain types of dermatitis and other inflamed skin conditions:

aspirin	animal serums	bromide
barbiturate	balsam	penicillin
quinine	thallium	sulphonamides
iodines	cortisone	salicylate
belladonna	bismuth	phenacetin

hydralazine drugs (used for high blood-pressure control).

Natural treatments

Herbs: Oil of evening primrose has proved successful for many skin condition sufferers. This oil has a rich content of linolenic acid, one of the essential fatty acids. Back in 1933, it was first reported that children with eczema have a low level of unsaturated fatty acids in their blood, and more recently, linolenic acid has been linked with eczema improvements. The department of dermatology of Bristol Royal Infirmary has compared its effects with placebo in 17 children and 15 adults suffering from 'atopic' eczema, ie., the commonest type of dermatitis, usually starting in childhood and often with a tendency to run in families. 'A modest but significant improvement' was reported by the doctors, based on the views of the group themselves and an independent doctor's assessment. The way the oil could help is not understood, but may be due to the essential fatty acid being required for production of a prostaglandin the body uses to protect itself. Some people may be unable to turn the supply of essential fatty acids from food into the material for making the prostaglandins. Others may not obtain enough linolenic acid from refined diets.

Other pure plant oils may also have a helpful effect, notably those high in essential fatty acids. A few capsules per day of safflower oil, or a dessertspoonful of wheat germ oil, safflower oil, linseed oil or sunflower seed oil are recommended. The so-called 'blood cleansing' herbs may help. An infusion of burdock, nettles or figwort would be worth trying, making into a strong 'tea', then taking a small glassful in three gulps each day. You will have to team this with dietary and other treatments which may have caused the complaint, the herbs serving to strengthen the body's recuperative power.

Supplements: You are unlikely to be short of all the 'vitamin cocktail' that follows, but it's well worth trying its effect:

> 1 vitamin A, capsule or tablet, 750IU
> 1 vitamin E, natural source, 50mg
> 1 vitamin C, 250mg
> 2 vitamin B_{12}
> 1 B complex

You may be able to find most of these items combined into a multivitamin/mineral supplement. Take three a day, with food. As with all natural treatments, be patient, as several weeks may be required before improvement is achieved. Skin ailments are often obstinate and do not respond readily. But the rule is that as the health improves, the skin improves.

Relaxation: Dermatitis and eczema are frequently worsened, although rarely solely caused, by anxiety and reaction to stress. This is why extra B vitamins and vitamin C, both likely to be used in greater quantities when stressed, may be effective. The skin complaint may not be easy to connect to stress: it may only occur after a long period of tension, when the body systems are depressed. By this time, you may be feeling happy with life, so fail to realize why your skin is reacting, showing that your body has not yet recovered fully.

Your body should produce antibodies which counteract harmful substances — foods or allergenic non-foods — that get inside the body. A good supply of antibodies will only be produced when vitamin C is generously supplied. Stress will cause you to use more vitamin C — hence the reduction in resistance. The amount of vitamin C necessary to correct the problem will vary with the individual. Our 'vitamin cocktail' supplies 750mg a day. Healthy meals should supply a further 100mg at least. You may prefer to 'up' your supplement to one gram per day. Do not start taking more than this without qualified supervision. The extra is unlikely to be harmful, but may if continued for a long time 'train' the body to expect a level of vitamin C which cannot be obtained from food. If you then stop taking the supplement, you may find that you suffer apparent vitamin C deficiency symptoms, even though your food may supply amounts usually plentiful.

Food allergy remains the first route to try. In a 1978-reported study, for instance, a double-blind trial with 20 children suffering between the ages of two and eight, showed that four weeks on a soya bean milk substitute, which the families thought was milk, produced improvement in eczema in 13 of the children. When the children took an identical-seeming product which in fact included dried milk and egg for another four weeks, six deteriorated. On the milk-free weeks (and neither children, parents or doctors knew which 'milk substitute' contains soya and which the egg-and-milk mixture), some children also needed fewer antihistamine drugs, slept better and were relieved of pruritus (anal itching). Of course, the children had to avoid foods containing either milk or eggs as foods for the whole of the trial.

5

Diseases of the Skin:
Internal Causes and Remedies

Unlike the causes just discussed, many skin problems are caused by internal disturbances, most of which can be helped if not removed by our own efforts. The following list will deal mainly with those problems of the skin which are not usually related to general diseases. So we don't talk about chickenpox, which definitely produces a temporary skin problem, but one which goes away when the chicken pox does. We *will* deal with such complaints as acne, chilblains and cold sores, which often appear to arrive out of the blue, but which are best tackled by changes in living habits.

Acne
When the sebaceous glands produce too much sebum, the natural skin lubricant, the pores through which it reaches the skin surface can become blocked, particularly where there are hair follicles or sweat glands. The resulting 'plug' of sebum can easily become infected with bacteria, in which case a typical acne pimple will form. The three main acne signs are three stages of this process:

Whiteheads: blocked up sebum under the skin.
Blackheads: blocked up sebum where the end of the pore is open although plugged. The black is not due to dirt. It is the result of the chemical reaction between the sebum and oxygen.

Pustules: where sebum has become infected with bacteria.

The over-production of sebum is strongly associated with changes in hormonal activity mainly in teenage and early 20's years, in both sexes. But it can't be either assumed that it will automatically clear up in a year or two, or blamed entirely on hormones. Some people continue to suffer, both from the complaint itself or from scarring. Telling a sufferer that it's 'natural' is both infuriating and perhaps misleading, when acne can often be controlled effectively without drugs.

Although antibiotic and steroid drugs are often used to treat acne, both have strong drawbacks which sufferers should be aware of before relying on them, particularly for long-term use. Use of antibiotics can be depressing, encourage 'rebound' attacks if medication is stopped, and build up resistance so that the drug becomes ineffective. Steroid creams may seem to relieve symptoms, but if you stop using them, symptoms may well return as the cause is not checked. However, long term use of steroid ointments is not safe. It can cause dry, flaky skin of a changed texture which never returns to normal, and can affect the ability of the adrenal glands, vital to several everyday functions, to work without the drug. Even the washes often used by acne sufferers can be counter-productive. Although cleanliness is important in controlling acne, preparations that 'clean' all the natural lubrication off the skin can simply stimulate it to produce more sebum. This is even more likely if the cleanser used is too alkaline in its chemical balance to match the natural acidity of the skin surface. If you wash off this so-called 'acid mantle', the skin will quickly try to replace its protective, anti-bacterial 'cloak' by producing more sebum.

For these reasons, avoid soap or strong astringents.

Instead, cleanse the face with a soapless bar, several brands of which are now available at good chemists. Pick one which claims to be 'acid-balanced'. Otherwise, follow washes with a very diluted rinse with cider vinegar — say 1 tablespoon to a glass of water. Nobody knows exactly what causes acne to break out in one young person, while another is unaffected. However, the following treatments have worked for many people:

Natural treatments

Food: For the general skin-food plan, see page 63.

Supplements: The two elements that have been shown to be most useful in skin conditions are *zinc* and *vitamin A*. Best food sources of zinc are seafood, such as oysters or shellfish, or herrings, followed by meat, whole grains, nuts, peas and beans. A lot of zinc eaten fails to be absorbed across the intestinal wall. To get a better supply, use *chelated zinc* supplements, where the zinc is surrounded by protein which prevents it forming an unabsorbable compound with something else in food before your body has a chance to use it.

In the UK, zinc supplements are limited to providing 4mg per day of actual zinc. Many zinc supplements don't list the actual zinc, but the amount of zinc compound which is very different. 100mg of zinc sulphate, for instance, yields 40mg of zinc; 100mg of zinc orotate, 17mg of zinc; 100mg of zinc, 14mg of zinc. Clinical biochemist Len Mervyn suggests that taking 15mg per day of zinc would be a suitable amount for combating acne. This is about the estimated daily requirement for an adult, and when partnered with a zinc-rich natural food diet, should be enough.

How can zinc help? The function of zinc in acne is poorly

understood, except that zinc is an essential ingredient of many enzymes, which act as 'triggers' for daily functions. If you eat large amounts of unprocessed bran, you may absorb zinc less well as it may combine with the phytic acid present. This does not apply to anything like the same degree when wholemeal bread and other unrefined cereals are eaten, as phytic acid tends to be broken down during fermentation and cooking. Zinc competes with copper in the body, so an excess of copper, from water pipes or cooking equipment could limit the body's zinc level. Processed foods tend to be low in zinc — and high in teenage eaters. Zinc falls to a lower level in women a week before a period, and some women suffer skin disturbances only at this time. It tends to be lower in women taking oral contraceptives, and some other drugs which are taken over a long period, such as anti-epilepsy medicines. It may be that zinc is a factor in one or more of the body functions affecting production of sebum.

Vitamin A has been used with success in some acne cases. One possible reason why was already being suggested in 1943, when Dr J. V. Straumfjord wrote in *Northwest Medicine*: 'Growth may be the most important aspect of puberty responsible for the development of acne. During cellular multiplication, the amount of vitamin A in each resultant cell will decrease unless there is a concomitant and proportionate increase in the supply of vitamin A to the growing tissue. Processes which lead to tissue growth may thus increase the local need for vitamin A.' Dr Straumfjord tested the value of vitamin A on 100 sufferers from acne. After taking vitamin A daily for six months and over, 79 patients became free or almost free from eruptions. Only three cases found no improvement.

Vitamin A-rich foods are: oily fish, butter, milk, eggs, dark green vegetables, carrots, peas, dried apricots, prunes, tomatoes and yellow fruit such as papayas. The first four sources listed supply one form of vitamin A, retinol, while the others mainly provide a precursor of the vitamin, carotene. For acne sufferers, it is the retinol type that seems most useful. The normal daily vitamin A requirement is 2500 daily units, equivalent to 0.75mg. Acne sufferers may benefit from taking a daily supplement of this amount or more. Don't take more unless you are under qualified supervision, as vitamin A can be stored by the body, so an excess is not necessarily excreted. Large excesses (so large that you would have to take many tablets or capsules each day) have been shown to have bad effects on health. However, you cannot obtain an overdose from a supplement provided you follow the instructions on the label and eat well too. Fresh foods are best, as although neither carotene nor retinol is damaged by cooking except by frying at very high temperatures (over 100°C), they are partially destroyed by exposure to light, for example, in bottled foods including doorstep milk.

Vitamin C may be helpful, along with B complex if acne flares up at times of stress. A typical amount to take might be 500mg of vitamin C per day, and a B complex at the dose indicated on the label.

Herbs: Burdock, clivers and figwort.

Other measures

Many acne sufferers find that exposure to sunlight relieves the condition. If sun is not available, a sunlamp may be used, providing ultra-violet light. This should be used under the direction of a practitioner, as it is easy to overdo exposure. Good ventilation of the skin affected helps too. This means that when the back and shoulders are affected, for instance, loose clothes should be worn made from natural fibres where possible. Don't squeeze or prick pustules. Blackheads can be pressed out gently after softening the surrounding skin with a hot water compress. Exercise is often avoided by acne sufferers, both because they fear it may encourage sebum production, and to avoid showing their skin by wearing sports clothes. But exercise can help normalize body functions, and stimulate elimination of sebum. After exercise, use a warm rather than hot shower or bath, followed by a cooler rinse, then pat dry.

Boils and Carbuncles

Boils are also known as furuncles. They are infections of the hair follicle by common skin bacteria. The infection is usually local. The infection produces a 'hard core' of pus, made up of bacteria plus dead white corpuscles which the body has used to restrict the infection. The size of the 'core' causes a painful swelling around it where the skin is squashed by the core. If the body defences are low, the infection may spread, producing a tender and enlarged lymph gland in your armpit or groin. A carbuncle is deeper-seated than a boil, occurring where there is a cluster of boils. It is flatter and when it discharges, will do so from several openings. Carbuncles often occur in the nape of the neck. Their effects are less local, often producing general illness. Diabetics are vulnerable to boils and carbuncles if their blood sugar is poorly controlled. Recurrent boils can be a sign of diabetes, so persistent sufferers should seek medical tests. However, in general both boils and carbuncles are signs of being 'rundown', or under stress.

Natural treatments

Food: As a general eating plan on page 63.

Supplements: As for acne. Garlic oil capsules or hot boiled onions can be applied to the boil.

Herbs: Burdock.

Other measures
As with acne, washing off the protective acid coating of the skin with alkaline soap makes it easier for infections to get a foothold. Avoid soap in favour of soapless washbars from chemists. Applying kaolin or magnesium sulphate paste helps draw out the pus. Hot water poultices can speed the development of the boil(s) if applied several times a day during the swollen stage. Anything that stimulates excretion and circulation is useful — see the notes in opening chapters about the value of exercise, water therapy and high-fibre food. If boils are connected with reaction to stress, develop relaxation methods (see notes on page 45).

Chilblains
Swollen, itchy, red and uncomfortable patches on toes and in worse cases, fingers, are a direct effect of cold feet or hands. The still unsolved mystery is why some people are so vulnerable to them, while others never suffer. This is not yet understood, although in theory, it is the effect of how good a person's circulation in the small surface blood vessels is. While waiting for a full explanation, here are the best measures known:

Natural treatments

Food: As general eating plan, with special attention to iron intake, as this is important for good circulation.

Supplements: The only supplement thought to be useful

is nicotinic acid, also known as vitamin B_3. This is a vasodilator, or in other words, it expands the blood vessels, allowing for better circulation in the chilblain areas. Your doctor should prescribe this.

NB. When you take it, expect to have a 'hot flush' lasting about 20-30 minutes, as the blood vessels expand, allowing extra blood to rush to the skin surface. It is harmless, but suggests that nicotinic acid is best taken in private.

Herbs: Ginger or chilli, both to stimulate circulation.

Other aids

The best way of avoiding chilblains is simply not to get cold feet or hands. The two main steps are to wear enough clothing, preferably of natural fabrics; and to wear it loose enough not to impede the blood flow. Central heating has already done a lot to reduce chilblains, and general warm temperatures are more effective than huddling up to a fire. Exercise will help boost circulation too, by encouraging deep breathing. When you wash, towel feet vigorously, or brush with a soft brush. For relief of chilblains, use homoeopathic black bryony (available as an ointment) or marshmallow cream.

Cold Sores

A good example of a skin condition that many sufferers consider unrelated to anything else. In fact, cold sores are a symptom of the *herpes simplex* virus, closely related to the *herpes zoster* virus that causes shingles, to the virus that causes chicken pox and to a similar virus that causes genital herpes. Once contracted, the *herpes simplex* virus is thought to lie dormant in the skin, until for some reason, it becomes active. Nobody understands why cold sores come and go unexpectedly, so the best guard is to maintain the body's defence system as well as you can. The small blister sores filled with clear fluid are not dangerous, but they can be catching if the person you are in contact with is also vulnerable to the virus. For any eruption more serious than the cold sore, seek qualified medical help: eyes can be permanently affected by a bad case of shingles, and the illness can be both distressing and long-lasting.

Natural treatments

Food: Resistance-building general healthy meals, see page 67. However, there is some evidence from America that herpes sufferers (all varieties) may also benefit by boosting their food's content of lysine, one of the essential proteins or amino acids in food. Lysine-rich foods are: fish, chicken, milk, cheese and beans. Doctors Arthur Norins, Richard Griffith and Christopher Kagan report 43 out of 45 of a group of sufferers from facial and genital herpes found relief from pain and from new attacks when they took 315 to 1200 extra milligrams of lysine per day. Eating 300g of fresh or tinned fish, or 400g of chicken, or 300ml of milk plus a good helping of beans would provide the extra lysine required.

Dr Griffith and his colleagues say that experience with hundreds of other patients shows that lysine works as well or better on genital herpes as on cold sores, with relief of pain the most dramatic effect. Patients must avoid nuts, chocolate and peanuts, all of which are rich in arginine, another amino acid which seems to help the herpes virus thrive. Once patients have got over a bout of herpes, the doctors suggest that 500mg of extra lysine a day can prevent new attacks.

Supplements: Where cold sores reflect a rundown condition, a general multi-vitamin/mineral supplement is sensible. In addition, naturopaths usually recommend large doses of vitamin B complex, with vitamin B_{12} especially important. Six daily kelp tablets will also ensure good mineral supplies. Lysine can be bought in tablets (eg. *Dermatabs*). Homoeopathic remedies include Rhus. Tox.6X in tablets or cream; Natrum Mur.6X.

Herbs: Herbs that stimulate circulation, or 'heating herbs', such as ginger (in hot drinks with lemon and honey), chilli and capsicum.

Other treatments
Local application of marshmallow ointment can be soothing. Methylated spirits will help sores dry quickly.

Dandruff
Once again, not just a local problem, dandruff or *seborrheic dermatitis* of the scalp, usually suggests a general rundown condition. The exceptions are where dandruff is the skin's reaction to some contact with material it doesn't like. The first steps in tackling dandruff include checking shampoo (harsh medicated ones can often set off reactions), hairslides, earrings, new face creams and other possible local irritants. Dandruff can also be linked to eczema (see under that heading).

Once you accept that dandruff is not just a local condition, but a reflection of body health, then it's obvious that anti-dandruff shampoos can't 'cure' the problem. They may relieve it (see Other treatments).

Natural treatments

Food: General healthy eating plan, as on page 63. Naturopaths blame dandruff on eating too many starchy and sugary foods, and not enough vitamin and mineral-rich foods.

Supplements: If dandruff coincides with feeling run down, a vitamin/mineral supplement is sensible.

Other treatments
Get plenty of fresh air, both to give your scalp ventilation and to stimulate circulation with exercise. You can boost scalp circulation by massaging the scalp with your fingertips to stimulate and to loosen up tension that often develops there. Use only mild shampoos, and follow with a rinse of either lemon juice or cider vinegar, 2 tablespoonsful to a glass of water. This can help keep the acidity of the scalp, which shampoos tend to break down. Find a shampoo that is acid-alkaline balanced — it will say 'pH-balanced' on the label. This is more likely to be an American brand.

Rosemary is a well known treatment for hair problems, and stinging nettles can also be used. With Rosemary, you can use natural shampoos including rosemary, or one of the following: leave sprigs of rosemary in olive oil for several weeks. Then rub a little into the scalp about 30 minutes or as long as possible before shampooing. Or buy rosemary oil, mix half and half with vegetable oil, and rub a few drops in with your final rinse. Or make a rosemary or nettle 'decoction', by bringing at least 25g of the herb to the boil in 300ml of water, slowly. Leave to simmer for several minutes, use when cold or warm. Give your hair a final rinse with some of this.

Dermatitis — see eczema

Eczema or dermatitis
External causes for dermatitis are discussed in the introductory chapters. They include washing powder, nickel reactions, cosmetics and many other irritants. A tendency to be sensitive to such influences can be

hereditary. The same is true of internal causes, and a sign of the hereditary influence is that the dermatitis will often be accompanied by hay fever, asthma or catarrh. However, there are natural treatments which have proved effective for many people who have resigned themselves to years of drugs or to being told they just have to live with the condition. Drugs can themselves worsen the condition, with skin eruptions one of the most common side-effects of many prescribed medicines.

Natural treatments

Look for external causes first, especially if the eczema is new. The next step is to look for possible foods that could be causing reactions. With children, the obvious foods to suspect are dairy products, followed by eggs, wheat-containing foods, oranges and fish. If there is a history of eczema in a family, bottle-feeding may be the first suspect as a possible cause of milk allergy. If this or another allergy exists, there is no point in cutting down on the food to see whether the problem improves. Even a small amount of the substance may set off a reaction, so you will only see results if you stop eating it completely. In the case of milk, this means no milk of any kind, alone or in cooking, in yogurt, cheese, ice cream, margarine (which usually contains whey from milk unless it is kosher margarine), butter or anything else containing milk. You may find that even if cow's milk is the culprit, goat's milk and even cow's milk in a different form, such as yogurt, can be tolerated. But to start with, no milk is a more useful rule.

Food allergy tests can be carried out by a specialist to whom your doctor refers you. Or you can do them at home. The basic method is simple. You stop even the smallest amount of the suspect food for about a week or 10 days.

By that time, any symptoms caused by that food should have become noticeably improved. At this point, you may 'test' by eating some of the food, and watching for reactions. This is not quite as easy as it sounds. Firstly, knowing that you are doing something about your condition may produce a temporary improvement which is a direct result of your mind — the so-called placebo effect. This is not to be scoffed at, as it does illustrate what a powerful influence our mind can have on our body, but it's unlikely to be lasting relief. Secondly, when you test by re-introducing the food, your mind may convince you that it is making you feel ill — even if there is no physical reaction caused by the food itself. A third problem is that the bad reaction to a food may take some time to develop, so confusing the connection between food and reaction. For this reason, if you re-introduce a food that your symptoms seem to have benefitted from the absence of, allow one or two days before changing the rest of your meals at all, to see if you can spot a reaction.

If you have no idea which food might be causing an adverse reaction, the testing procedure may take a tediously long time, as you should only exclude one food at a time, then starting eating it if no improvement occurs, while you exclude the next suspect. To speed the process, allergy tests are often done by reducing all food eaten by the sufferer to two items, plus spring or mineral water, for about five days. During this time, usually spent eating lamb and pears, or cod and peas, health should improve. Then one new food only is introduced each day until the suspect, producing bad reactions, is confirmed.

To shorten this still-boring method, always test first for the most common foods which people cannot tolerate — ie., milk products, wheat products, eggs, coffee, tea and chocolate. Test first for your favourite foods, as it often seems to be the foods for which we have the strongest cravings that may be causing bad reactions. Also see the address list for useful self-help associations. But what if you are unable to find any connection between your dermatitis and food? Or between it and any other potential external irritant, such as metal or fumes?

Food: Use the general regime on page 67. However, if you suffer from any form of catarrh, sinus trouble, hay fever or asthma in addition to your skin condition, you may well benefit by making the following adjustments — even if you are not allergic to the foods concerned:

● Eating too many dairy foods can encourage the production of excess mucus, blocking up the breathing passages.

● Eating too much starch — even of the unrefined kind such as wholemeal bread, can also cause some people's mucus-lined nasal passages to clog up.

● Cut down on both these, without cutting them out. Instead, eat more fruit and vegetables, in all kinds of forms. Use potatoes in preference to grains, ie., choose a baked jacket potato rather than a sandwich, or have potatoes or other root vegetables with a meal, rather than eating bread, pasta or another form of grain.

6

Exercise and Diet

Some skin problem sufferers are reluctant to exercise because they have one of these reactions:

1. Psoriasis and some dermatitis sufferers sometimes experience a flare-up after sun on the skin.
2. Swimming can be embarrasing for severe eczema, psoriasis or acne sufferers. Some other sufferers also avoid swimming pools, as the chlorine and drying effect make their skin feel worse.
3. Heavy sweating can aggravate spots in some acne sufferers.
4. If sport leads to lots of washing and hair washing, skin can become dry, and dermatitis or eczema can worsen.

Problems such as these should not put you off exercise. Here are some of the ways round such problems:

1. If sunlight affects you, choose an indoor sport, from table tennis or badminton, to squash or yoga. In sunshine, simply cover up. Equally many skin sufferers find that sunshine improves their condition.
2. The drying effect of swimming pools can be partly offset by not using soap when showering afterwards, but just lots of water, followed by some sort of lotion that will keep the skin's natural oils in. You can also

cover yourself with barrier cream before swimming.

3. The flush of blood to the skin after exercise is very good for skin conditions. If you find that spots result, try a cool shower after an exercise, followed by a brisk towelling. This will help the body dispose of waste products quickly. Wearing well ventilated clothes is important too. The spots result because pores are blocked: improving circulation and ventilation will help.

4. Don't accompany sport with lots of soap and shampoo — both dry out the skin. Just pile on the water, and use the gentlest of products. This means those with acid-balanced contents, so that they don't upset the natural acid-alkali balance of the skin, and without strong perfumes or other ingredients. Soap and washing powders are both common causes of dermatitis.

The best exercises for skin conditions are:

1. Those which improve circulation, ie., anything which makes you hot. This can range from *brisk* walking, especially up and down hill, to dancing or skipping. It's essential to let the air get at the skin, and to breathe deeply. So weight training or isometrics would not be as useful.

2. Those which tone up the general system, ie., almost any exercise which uses the body fully. So swimming, cycling and walking would be excellent, but golf, snooker or bowling are not so useful.

   It's better to have several short exercise sessions a week, than one weekly heavy session, which is less effective in building up stamina or improving general health.

   General body fitness will help ensure that it is not unfit organs that are provoking skin symptoms.

Even housebound people can take exercise. Dancing, exercise routines with or without music, skipping, and yoga are all available any time. Yoga does not make you hot and breathless, but lays a lot of stress on breathing — an important part of improving circulation.

Eating for Your Skin and General Health

The same foods that help general good health will also be best for skin condition. See under individual ailments to find details of particular foods associated with causing or relieving the problem. These guidelines do not take into account individual food intolerances, as these do not mean that this food is not a healthy one for everyone else. Instead, the guidelines concentrate on the foods that provide the body with most nutrients, so that it has the 'raw material' for all it needs — and on avoiding foods that are not nutritious enough to be useful, and which can be positively harmful in excess. For most people the guidelines do not mean giving up all favourite foods — just changing the routine so that some are eaten more and others less. After a while, you should find that your tastes have changed towards the healthier pattern because you find it suits you better.

The basic aims:

● **To eat as little sugar as possible** — up to 25g per day, compared with the average of 100g per person per day. Sugar in fruit is not restricted, because you get other nutrients with it. In other sugars, you get only calories (plus some trace minerals in brown sugars). Sugar's high calorie content (110 per 25g) not only makes it easy to get or stay overweight, it also means that sugar-lovers fail to eat the other foods that would provide the vitamins, minerals and fibre their body and skin need. Sugar is also an essential element in tooth decay. The body does not need *any* crystal sugar. Energy can be produced just as effectively from other foods.

● **To eat more fruit and vegetables** — which provide large amounts of the vitamin C and other vital vitamins, minerals and fibre on which the body and skin can thrive. The fibre helps elimination, so avoiding the skin's eliminative powers being overstrained. As much produce as possible should be eaten raw, so that all its nutritive value is maintained. Growing your own, or buying the freshest produce available and eating it quickly, is a better investment in health than any bottle of tonic. Eat the extra fruit and vegetables instead of more concentrated foods like some of the dairy foods, bread, biscuits, meat, etc., you eat now. Your system and skin will both appreciate the easier work.

● **Eat less fat** — both animal and vegetable, but cutting down more on any hard kind of fat, from lard to lamb. We all need some fat, but only about half as much as most of us eat. The rest helps us gain weight easily — as fat has twice as many calories as protein or carbohydrate, per gram; it's hard to digest; excess fat is linked with many long-term health disorders, particularly of circulation, that may have skin symptoms.

Unlike sugar, we do need some fat — but most of us would feel far less clogged up *and* be more prudent to eat much less. To cut down, avoid fried foods, heavy layers of butter or margarine or adding these to vegetables or potatoes; favour roast and grilled recipes; dodge hidden fats in pastry, cheese, chocolate, etc. Make the fats you do use the best quality: for animal fats, that means the oily fish, which have essential fatty acids, plus plenty of vitamins A and D. For vegetable oils, choose soft ones or liquid oils. Pick only margarines high in polyunsaturates, and use the oils richest in polyunsaturates — both being the best sources of essential fatty acids. The three main oils are safflower, sunflower and soya. Because polyunsaturated fats are unstable under high temperatures, don't fry with these, but use corn or olive oil — but then, fry less and use less oil.

● **Eat more fibre** — which will help your skin by helping your body eliminate the waste products of food and metabolism. Eating more fibre means both cereal fibre, and the kinds of fibre in fruit and vegetables. As cereal fibre occurs in unrefined cereals, such as wholemeal bread, when you eat more of these, you will also be getting more vitamins and minerals lost when fibre is refined away. So you'll also be improving the supply of other nutrients the body needs.

Some people are nervous of eating more wholemeal bread, cereals, pulses, potatoes and other sources of unrefined fibre, because they think they will gain weight. In fact, by eating less sugar and fat, you can save far more calories than you will 'spend' on unrefined carbohydrates. Carbohydrates have no more calories than proteins, nor any special 'fattening' ability. For example if you eat 25g less of sugar (110 calories) and 25g less of fat (average 225 calories) in a day, you will save 335 calories, or the equivalent of over 125g of wholemeal bread, or over 325g of potatoes. These foods will give you many more vitamins and minerals as well as fibre and energy, and proteins.

● **Eat less salt** — one of the products the skin has most to do with, as you will realize from the saltiness of sweat. Most Westerners eat at least three to five times as much salt as they need, so that even serious athletes who sweat a lot rarely benefit from extra. Instead, excess salt makes the kidneys overwork, and can encourage high blood pressure. High blood pressure is a recognized sign of extra risk of both heart attack and stroke. Salt isn't the only factor, but one of the most avoidable. By eating more fruit and vegetables, you help supply the balancing element to salt, potassium.

Following these guidelines, you can be confident that every nutrition expert, orthodox or not, will agree that you are doing the best you can for your system. That is, all these steps are free from controversy among experts, as everyone agrees on them. In the process, you will find you use far fewer ready-made foods, which has the associated benefit of meaning you eat fewer additives. These can be a source of skin upsets, see under eczema. However, this style of eating need not entail more trouble in preparing meals, and usually costs less. This is because the fresh food way involves more fresh fruit and vegetable dishes, which are generally easy and quick to make.

Diets That Bring Results
As well as switching to the pattern of eating that helps general health (see page 63), sufferers from skin problems may like to take more rapid steps towards recovery by using a special diet for a week or more.

1. In cases of acne, boils and mild skin problems, the sufferer can go on an all-fruit diet for five to seven days, then on the regular healthy eating plan.

2. For carbuncles, eczema, more serious dermatitis, psoriasis or shingles, a fruit juice fast can be followed for three days. Do not fast for longer unless under qualified supervision. Do not fast without qualified advice if you are taking drugs, including prescribed

medicines; if you have a heart condition; if you are diabetic; or if you have ulcers. For this type of fast, simply drink a glass of fruit or vegetable juice, diluted with mineral water if wished, every two hours. Extra glasses of mineral water can be added if wanted.

3. A week on this restricted diet followed by the '7-day pattern' will also help many sufferers.

Fruit diet

Morning: a glassful of diluted fruit juice, especially grapefruit juice. Unsweetened.

Midday: raw vegetable salad. Dessert: figs, raisins, prunes, dates or fresh fruit.

Evening: raw salad, plus one or two vegetables steamed, such as spinach, carrots, turnips, cauliflower, cabbage, etc. Dessert: fresh fruit.

7-day pattern

Day 1: Breakfast: diluted juice of 2 oranges; grapes; 1 apple.

Lunch: salad of lettuce, tomato, grated carrot and beetroot.

Wholemeal bread and butter or soft margarine.

A few raisins or dates.

Evening meal: poached egg on steamed spinach; steamed carrots and celery. Baked apple.

Day 2: Breakfast: soaked raisins; 1 orange; glass of yogurt.

Lunch: raw vegetable salad, made from as many salad vegetables as wished. Cottage cheese.

Wholemeal bread and butter or soft margarine.

Evening meal: Lamb chop or vegetable protein savoury; steamed cabbage, marrow, onion or leeks. Stewed fruit.

Day 3: Breakfast: fresh fruit salad. Yogurt (unsweetened).

Lunch: lettuce, celery, banana and date salad. Wholemeal bread and butter or soft margarine.

Evening meal: steamed fish or vegetarian savoury. Any two vegetables, steamed. Soaked dried fruit.

Day 4: Breakfast: 1 raw juicy seasonal fruit, one kind of dried fruit.

Lunch: poached egg on spinach, baked potato in its jacket, steamed green vegetable. Baked apple.

Evening meal: purée of vegetables. Salad of as many raw vegetables as wanted. Wholemeal bread and butter or soft margarine.

Day 5: Breakfast: 1 apple; a few soaked prunes; plain yogurt.

Lunch: mixed salad as wished. Wholemeal toast and butter or soft margarine. A pear or some grapes.

Evening meal: buttered cauliflower; steamed carrots; baked jacket potato. Grated nuts or grated cheese. Baked apple.

Day 6: Breakfast: half a grapefruit; grapes; 1 apple.

Lunch: raw vegetables salad; cottage cheese. Wholemeal bread and butter or soft margarine. A few raisins, dates or dried figs.

Evening meal: chicken; two or three steamed vegetables. Fresh fruit.

Do not use commercial salad dressings. Instead, use orange or lemon juice, or lemon juice and olive oil or plain yogurt with lemon juice.

An alternative breakfast is grated apple, yogurt and three dessertspoonsful of wheat germ with a few raisins.

Use as little salt as possible. This style of eating avoids most of the usual salt in meals because it uses natural rather than processed food. However, it is still worth only adding the minimum of salt both in cooking or at table.

Spread butter or margarine thinly. Only use margarines labelled 'high in polyunsaturates'. Some people like to mix butter and polyunsaturated margarine to gain taste without too many saturated fats.

Don't use ordinary tea or coffee, cola drinks or other soft drinks. Instead, drink diluted fruit or vegetable juice; mineral water; herb teas; decaffeinated coffee or low tannin teas.

You should find that this kind of eating pattern removes any tendency to constipation. If it does not, add a little bran to salads and cereal, starting with a cautious 2 teaspoonsful a day, as too much can make you feel bloated. Increase bran until you feel free from constipation, raising intake to 2 tablespoonsful a day gradually over several weeks or months. However, other foods in this regime also include fibre, so you may well find bran unnecessary.

One of the important features of this style of eating is to provide enough of the B vitamins. A shortage of almost any B vitamin will show in skin problems. Since this vitamin is water-soluble, and only stored by the body in small amounts (apart from vitamin B_{12}), you should make a point of eating good sources daily. These are: yeast, such as brewer's yeast; yogurt and cottage cheese; wholemeal bread; wheat germ; fish and meat.

You can also take B vitamins as a supplement. However, if you decide to take extra of a particular B vitamin, always take some B complex as well. This group of vitamins often inter-relate in the body. The simplest way of taking the complex in balance is to take yeast, either in powder or tablets. The powder is more concentrated, but most people do not like the flavour, preferring to swallow tablets rather than take something that stays in the mouth.

Food, as we have said, is not the only factor in self-help for skin problems. Nor are poor eating habits the sole cause. If you are taking steps to improve what you eat, don't neglect the two other vital points: exercise and relaxation. All three work together.

Your other weapon must be persistence, since skin problems are only occasionally 'overnight arrivals'. In other cases, they have appeared over a long period following years of living habits which the sufferer's individual nature cannot cope with. It may take months, or even a year or two in the case of obstinate problems such as psoriasis, to achieve results.

However, don't doubt that success can be yours. Thousands of other people have got rid of their skin complaints by all-natural means — and in the process, improved their general health. This is the big attraction of this form of treatment. Remember that skin problems usually mean internal problems, and that the measures you are taking, however tedious they may sometimes seem, are not only improving your skin, but your whole vitality and health prospects for many far more grave illnesses.

7

Water Therapy

Water therapy is a natural and traditional way of helping the skin in two ways: improving its circulation, which in turn helps it obtain all the nourishment it needs to counteract any skin problem; and helping the body rid itself of waste products via the skin that might otherwise be retained and make skin problems worse.

Water therapy, also known as hydrotherapy, has two main parts. By immersion alternatively in hot and then cold water, the blood is driven to and then away from the surface. The small capillary blood vessels are dilated and contracted. The result: stimulation of circulation. The second method used is friction. When the skin is wet or under water, it can be rubbed or brushed more briskly, without hurting. Hot water encourages the pores to open (as does exercise), aiding the disposal of waste products. Cold water and friction both stimulate the supply of blood, as the body sends extra blood to the area to warm it up again. Water therapy does not need to be on the site of skin problems: as we've said, underlying those problems is often a general body imbalance, which the water treatment may help the body put right.

Please note that water therapy should not involve soap. Soap should be treated with suspicion by sufferers of skin ailments. Because most soap recipes produce an alkaline product, it can upset the natural 'acid mantle' atmosphere of the skin, causing drying, itching and scaling in many people. Soap can't help but remove the natural oils which protect the skin — and however well advertised its formula, nothing can replace that protection. In some people, soap is the cause of dermatitis, either via its detergent agent, or via other ingredients used. This is even more true of washing powders, especially the 'biological' type. Use gloves when handling, and if you are sensitive, change to a different type of powder.

Ways of Using Water to Help Your Skin

1. The most traditional form of water treatment, recommended by all kinds of natural healers, is a cool shower each day, followed by a brisk rubdown with a fairly rough towel. The shower can be cool or cold, depending how you feel, but the colder the better. It does not have to be long, just enough to cool the skin enough to encourage the body to send extra blood to the area. The result is that this kind of shower is invigorating, rather like the sensation after a swim — which of course can fulfil the same function.

2. Sitz baths are another traditional treatment, where hot and cold water are alternated. Doctors often recommend something like this for chilblains, dipping the feet alternately in hot and cold water. The effect on the whole body is just as beneficial to circulation. You need two large washing-up type tubs. Fill one with water as hot as you can stand, the other with cold water. Put them in the bath, and sit in the hot water tub, with your feet in the cold water one, for three minutes. Then switch ends for one minute. Repeat two or three times, always finishing by sitting in the cold water. Then rub down briskly. Another way of doing this is to run a hot bath, in which you place a large tub of cold water resting on a low stool or support. You sit in the bath for three minutes, with your knees raised

so that only your pelvic region and feet are in the water. Then sit in the cold water for one minute, leaving your feet in the hot. Repeat two or three times, ending sitting in the cold water. Towel briskly.

3. Tepid baths can relieve itching — see also under psoriasis.

4. Baths can help relaxation, which as we've said, can be an important factor in some skin conditions. In this case, use water just around blood heat, ie., around 98-99°F/36-37°C. You can add an infusion of one or more of the herbs linked with relaxation: examples are valerian, chamomile or rosemary. Add 25g of dried herb, or 50g of fresh, to 600ml of water, bring to the boil and leave to infuse for 15 minutes, before removing herbs and adding liquid to bath. The essential oils from the herbs are the active component, giving off aromatic scents that, research suggests, affect the brain directly through breathing them in. The other benefit for relaxation is simply that taking a bath gives you a break. If you usually feel overwhelmed by tasks, a relaxing bath can help you put your thoughts in order and feel in control. Showers are excellent for cleansing without soap, and if you have good pressure, for providing a kind of water massage.

Useful Addresses

Self-help Associations

Action Against Allergy
43 The Downs
London SW20 8HG
01-947 5082

Food Allergy Association
c/o The Chairman, Mrs Ellen Rothera
27 Ferringham Lane
Ferring
West Sussex
0903 41178

National Eczema Society
Tavistock House North
Tavistock Square
London WC1H 9SR
01-388 4097

The Psoriasis Association
7 Milton Street
Northampton NN2 7JG
0604 711129

Chemical Victims
Club for allergy sufferers
Clinical Ecology Research Unit
Basingstoke District Hospital
Park Prewitt
Basingstoke
Hants
0256 3202

Hyperactive Childrens' Support Group
Also helpful on allergy and additive-free diets.
c/o Mrs I. Colquhoun
Mayfield House
Yapton Road
Barnham
E. Sussex
0243 551313

Alternative Practitioners

If you want to explore non-drug methods of treating skin conditions, a naturopath or a herbalist is the most likely practitioner to guide you. They can show you how food can be used as a treatment, help tackle the causes of the problem and not just the symptoms, and provide ideas for natural relief in the meantime. To find your nearest qualified practitioner write to:

British Naturopathic and Osteopathic Association
6 Netherhall Gardens
London NW3 5RR
01-435 8728

National Institute of Medical Herbalists
65 Frant Road
Tunbridge Wells
Kent
0892 27439

Before you visit a practitioner, write a short history of your complaint so that you know the timing, any associated circumstances and other details that may need checking, so that you can give a full story to help them help you more effectively. Remember that natural treatments often (not always) take some time, weeks rather than days, to work, especially if your condition is long-established. So be patient, reminding yourself that this form of treatment has the advantage of getting to the root of the problem, not just providing a temporary respite.

Glossary of Natural Skin Aids

Almond oil
A versatile oil, used in many natural cosmetic products, including facial creams and massage lotions. It's sold on its own for people who want to make up their own natural cosmetics, such as this Overnight Hand Treatment, to help troubled skin recover faster: Beat 1 egg yolk, blend in one tablespoonful of sweet almond oil, 1 teaspoonful of tincture of benzoin, 1 tablespoonful of rose water, in that order and mix thoroughly. Last thing before bed, rub the mixture into your hands, then put on a pair of loose gloves to save your sheets. The same mixture can be used externally to ease skin inflammations and itching.
Caution: a few people react badly to almond oil, especially used 'neat', ie., at full strength. Try a little on a small patch of skin 24 hours before going further.

Aloe vera
Extracted from a cactus-like plant that grows in America's southern desert areas, aloe vera is valued for its healing, soothing and moisturizing properties. It's a popular ingredient of all kinds of moisturizer, and especially of products to protect the skin from drying out in the sun. In such suntan products, it is often teamed with jojoba oil, from another desert plant, and PABA. You can't usually buy the oil by itself.

Apricot oil

Oil from the kernels of the apricot is often used in creams intended for older skins. It's claimed to be easily absorbed, and fine in texture.

Avocado

Avocado is considered useful for the skin because of the oil it contains. One way of using the fruit is in a mask for oily skins: Mash half a small avocado pear thoroughly with a teaspoonful of lemon juice (this stops it going brown and unappealing) and an egg white (which will have a tightening, astringent effect on the skin). After cleansing your face, smear on the mask and leave for about 15 minutes before washing off. Finish by rinsing face in cool water.

Azulene

An ingredient of chamomile, see below.

Bran

Mainly used for skin in two ways, similar to oatmeal: as a bath additive, to soothe inflammations, rashes, itches and abscesses; and as a dirt-absorbent, mildly abrasive wash. Traditional bran baths involve boiling 1kg of bran for 5 minutes, then straining the liquid into the bath (if you put the bran in the bath, you will guarantee a blocked drain). The bath water should be warm rather than hot, and the sufferer should stay immersed for 15-30 minutes. For use as a face wash, use the same mixture and technique described under Oatmeal.

Burdock

To describe burdock as a 'blood cleanser' may make it
sound like one of those cure-alls hawked round Victorian
fairs, but it is difficult for herbalists to sum up its properties
otherwise. The root can be used to help eczema, by making
a decoction: Simmer 25g of the chopped up root in 500ml
of water, covered, for 10 minutes. Use fresh root (it's a
common wild plant) if possible. Cool and strain; take a
tablespoonful twice a day for two or three days, then a
wineglassful a day. If using this treatment for eczema (it
is also a good general tonic), expect a flare-up for a few
days before the eczema gets better. This is a sign that the
burdock is encouraging the body to restore itself to health.

Cabbage

Cabbage compresses, made simply by applying pulped
cabbage leaves held on by a bandage, are a traditional
European remedy for bringing spots and boils to a head.
They are also used to relieve swellings. Savoy cabbage is
particularly recommended by top Swiss natural health
doctor, Alfred Vogel.

Chamomile

Chamomile is famous for the soothing, relaxant properties
of the tea made by pouring 500ml of boiling water over
25g of the herb. Externally, it's best known for encouraging
the blondeness of fair hair — using the same infusion as
above as a final rinse after shampooing. Its internal relaxing
properties can be extended to the skin, on which
chamomile can act as a soothing refresher. The agent in
chamomile credited with this effect is called azulene. To
make a refreshing skin compress, pour 125ml of boiling
water on to one heaped teaspoonful of the dried herb.

Leave to infuse for 10 minutes, dip cottonwool pads in warm liquid and cover closed lids for 5 to 10 minutes. Splash with cold water. Applying this compress all over the face may relieve acne. If using fresh chamomile, use three teaspoonsful of the flowers. A similar anti-swelling compress can be made with infusions of verbena, fennel, coltsfoot, eyebright or elderflowers.

Cider vinegar

Plain cider vinegar can be used on a cold compress for swollen veins, feet or ankles, or to relieve sunburn. Another way of using cider vinegar is to mix 500ml with 500ml of water in which 25g of rosemary has been simmered for ten minutes. This mixture can then be used as a skin tonic in place of harsh astringents, to refresh hot and oily skin or as a scalp rinse after shampooing.

Clay

Clay is often used in face masks, for instance, in the form of fullers earth. A typical recipe is: Mix one tablespoonful of fuller's earth with enough witchhazel to make a paste that will smooth on to the skin. Apply and relax for about 15 to 20 minutes, before washing off. Leave eye area free of mask, and cover with pads of cottonwool soaked in chamomile tea or in water, covering slices of cucumber. Wash off thoroughly. Clay can also be used to make a poultice with a hot herb infusion, the herb and clay acting together, for instance, with minced cabbage, clay and hot water. The paste, using about one tablespoonful of clay powder, is spread about 6mm thick on an inflamed area. It is advisable not to let it dry out, as it is then difficult to remove, so cover with a polythene strip. The poultice can be left on all night if wished. Clay poultices might be used for skin ulcers, skin swellings, boils or abcesses. Other herbs that might be used with them include infusions of burdock, marigold flowers or chamomile. These uses of clay are partly related to its ability to 'carry' other ingredients in such a way as to keep them in contact with the skin easily, or to its own dirt-absorbing and de-greasing power. Kaolin is the other common form of clay used, in similar ways. Cosmetics based on clay are now available.

Cocoa butter

A solid fat extracted from the cocoa bean, popular with makers of skincare products because, although it has a firm texture, it melts easily when it meets the warmth of the skin, and so goes smoothly and non-stickily over the face, even though the coating will be heavy enough to protect against moisture loss. Cocoa butter crops up most often in suntan preparations, where it often and confusingly meets coconut oil — another solid fat despite its name. Both are more like waxes than like butter. Cocoa butter is pleasant-smelling, too. It is also used in cleansing creams, and in hair conditioners. Until recently, cocoa butter was difficult to buy in small amounts for the individual to use at home. However, the growth in interest in home-made cosmetics means that you can often buy it at large chemists. An example of how it might be used is in this skin cream: Gently warm together equal weights of wheatgerm oil and cocoa butter, add a few drops of essential oil of chamomile, basil, rosemary or neroli. Mix until smooth. A handcream made with cocoa butter involves melting gently together a spoonful of strong chamomile tea, almond oil, and cocoa butter, in about equal amounts, then adding a small spoonful of lemon juice. Stir until smooth and cool. Use for improving the condition of hands and other skin.

Comfrey

Best known for its wound healing powers, attributed to an ingredient known as allantoin, comfrey is also used to help relieve inflamed skin conditions. Strong comfrey tea can be applied as a compress, or comfrey creams can be used, even if these are designed for vanity rather than healing. Many people consider that comfrey is a valuable aid to avoiding premature wrinkling.

Cucumber

A mild astringent, cucumber is a way of counteracting over-oily skin without producing an oily rebound as the skin reacts to the way that harsh astringents remove the oil on the skin. The simplest way to use it is just to wipe the skin with slices of cucumber after cleansing. Slices placed over the eyes, topped with pads of wet cottonwool to weight them down, are refreshing and can reduce puffiness.

Echinacea

Sometimes described as 'the herbalist's penicillin', echinacea is used both herbally and homoeopathically. Also known as the purple coneflower, this plant is native to Mexico and some other parts of America. It is used there to counter infection and inflammation, applied externally or swallowed. Tablets of echinacea are available in Britain, for internal use. On the like-cures-like principle, homoeopaths use echinacea to counter adverse reactions to penicillin. In relation to skin problems, echinacea is used wherever skin is inflamed or vulnerable to infection via a cut or wound. It can also be used internally to help the skin recover from acne infection, rashes or eczema outbreaks.

Eggs

Face masks often use eggs, which may be for their fat content, or more specifically for the waxy lecithin in the yolk. Egg yolk is usually intended to moisturize and lubricate the skin, egg white to tighten it (although this effect will only be temporary). Here's one egg mask: Mix one egg with one teaspoonful of honey and one of almond oil. Cover the face, leaving gaps round the eyes, and leave for 15-25 minutes while you relax, for instance in the bath. You can cover your eyes with pads of cottonwool soaked in something anti-inflammatory, such as cold tea, or with slices of cucumber. Rinse off with tepid water, then cooler water to finish.

Elderflowers

A long-popular cleanser consists of elderflower infusion, made by filling a jug with crushed flowers, topping with boiling water and then covering. Strain, then use in one of these ways. Add 500ml to the bath as a refreshing extra; soak pads of cotton or cottonwool in infusion and place on skin for about 20 minutes to soothe irritation or sunburn.

Evening primrose oil

Often taken internally to relieve eczema. It has also been found beneficial by some women in relieving their premenstrual syndrome — which might be useful to those whose skin complaints appear or worsen before a period.

Garlic

Mainly used on skin for its antiseptic properties, as it is used internally. To clean cuts and grazes, and discourage the development of bacteria in acne-spotted skin, garlic can be crushed and simply placed on the affected area under a bandage. Or vinegar in which crushed garlic has been left for a few weeks can be used to bathe the affected areas. A traditional ointment for skin conditions consists of cloves of garlic simmered until soft, then crushed and combined with the same quantity of honey. It's left on the skin overnight, covered with a loose wrapping of cotton or greaseproof paper, then washed off in the morning. The treatment is repeated for a few days. To bring boils or pimples to a head, rub with the cut side of a half clove of garlic, squeezing the clove so that juice flows on to the spot. For skin ailments, garlic may be beneficial inside and out.

Honey

Crops up in many skincare products, thanks to its repute as a skin softener and nourisher with the bonus of mild antiseptic properties. The last feature makes honey a popular ingredient in cleansing masks, especially if you have infected areas that need mild treatment. To make a mask suitable for oily skin or to treat large pores, mix two large tablespoonsful of yogurt (plain) with the same amount each of honey and oatmeal. Add enough strong fennel tea (made from teabag, or by adding two teaspoonsful of ground fennel seeds to half a cupful of boiling water, and leaving to 'stew'), to mix. You can grind the fennel seeds in a mortar or electric coffee grinder. Smear mixture on to face, and neck, leaving eye area and mouth clear. After 15-20 minutes of relaxation (ideally in the bath, so that drips won't matter), wash off with warm water, then rinse with cold water to finish. The fennel could be replaced by comfrey tea or chamomile tea. Comfrey would be better for dry skin, chamomile for greasier. Honey can also be used as a moisture-retainer, by mixing a little with a few drops of strong herb tea; or by mixing egg yolk with a teaspoonful of honey, a few drops of almond oil and a little herb tea.

Horsetail

It is the silica in horsetail that is credited with giving this garden 'weed' its ability to help in various skin problems. A decoction made by boiling the fresh herb in water (four tablespoonsful of chopped herb to 125ml water) for 10 minutes, then allowing to stand for 15 minutes before straining, is used in several ways. The most common is on pads of cottonwool as an eye compress to relieve soreness or inflammation. The same mixture also makes an anti-puffy face lotion. If you drink the tea in small amounts, it can act as a diuretic — de-puffing skin swollen by excess fluid that way; it is used herbally for this property and as a kidney stimulant. Silica is also used homoeopathically to treat boils, abcesses, excess offensive perspiration and wound or ulcer healing. It is often taken in conjunction with calcium. It is associated by homoeopaths with good skin condition. Two tablets of the 6x or 12x potency are recommended.

Jojoba

Oil from the jojoba plant has been greeted as a 'wonder oil'. That's partly because it provides the first satisfactory substitute for the oil of the sperm whale for manufacturers. The sperm whale is an endangered species, and by reducing demand for its oil, jojoba may help its survival. Many cosmetic buyers dislike the thought that their vanity could threaten animals. The other reason for this oil's increasing popularity with makers of skin products is its gentle, non-irritant moisturizing properties. Jojoba oil is sometimes used 'neat' on greasy skins to discourage the skin from producing too much sebum, the natural skin lubricant which in excess makes skin over-oily and acne-prone. Jojoba oil can be used as a cleanser, to help soften dry skin, as well as for soothing sensitive skin irritation.

Lanolin

One of the most common cosmetic ingredients, this is unfortunately a case which proves that 'natural' products can also cause adverse reactions. A sizeable number of people react with skin rashes to this oil from sheep's fleece. If you have ever had a bad skin reaction after using a product, especially a new product, lanolin may be the first suspect ingredient. As cosmetic ingredient labelling is not compulsory, you will have to write to the manufacturer to find out if lanolin is present. However, many products sold in health food stores either carry full ingredient labelling voluntarily, or guarantee freedom from any animal-derived ingredients, or say on the pack if lanolin has been included. Lanolin is used as a moisturizing ingredient in many face and body creams or lotions. If you want to make your own cosmetics, make sure that you don't react badly to lanolin, but using a little of some lanolin-carrying product on a small patch of the skin first. You can do this by visiting the cosmetics department of a large store, and looking round to find a product provided for sampling which contains lanolin. There are two main types of lanolin, one with water added, known as 'hydrous', and one without, 'anhydrous'. Anhydrous lanolin, available at many chemists, is best for making moisturizing creams that are rich in texture.

Lecithin

Taking lecithin internally has been linked with relief of psoriasis, one of the most stubborn and mysterious of skin ailments, (see page 34). The word comes from lekithos, the Greek for egg yolk, which was the first discovered source. The properties of lecithin are seen when you make mayonnaise: lecithin is an emulsifier, enabling watery and oily substances to mix. The oil can be separated into tiny globules that will stay suspended in non-oily substances. Most lecithin sold as a supplement is derived from soya bean oil, although egg lecithin and sunflower lecithin are also sold: there's no known superiority of any one type. The emulsifying properties of lecithin have led to its association with reducing blood fat levels and the tendency to build up fatty deposits which can block the arteries. Food processors use lecithin for its emulsifying properties, for instance in confectionery.

Lemon

Astringent and so mainly used to tighten and refresh oily skin but never undiluted. Mix with mineral water, using about a tablespoonful of lemon juice to 125ml of water. If used to remove last traces of cleanser, this will also restore natural acidity to the skin — as would vinegar. This can often help flaky skin and eczema, or limit perspiration from over-sweaty feet. The juice of a lemon diluted with very hot water, drunk first thing on waking, is a habit many people swear by for solving constipation and generally feeling well and indirectly aids skin. You can use the same mixture, perhaps with a teaspoonful of honey, as an effective nightcap. Other people combine two teaspoonsful of cider vinegar with a honey-lemon mixture and hot water to make a hot drink that has a slightly antiseptic quality — so may help sore throats or 'one-degree-under' moods.

Don't forget that the lemon juice, if freshly squeezed, is also rich in vitamin C. Some people find that dabbing lemon juice on a developing cold sore prevents the blistering. However, you have to dab repeatedly through the day, and catch it early. Others use cider vinegar for the same purpose.

Lemon juice is used in face masks both for its astringent and its whitening effect. If avocado is used, lemon juice stops it going brown and mushy. Used halved lemons can be rubbed quickly over your elbows, an area which often discolours; or over your hands, to help keep them white. A lemon juice mask involves mixing a teaspoonful of lemon juice with a tablespoonful of plain yogurt and a teaspoonful of bran. Add more yogurt if needed to make a thick paste which is rubbed into the skin so that the bran particles can collect dirt and by their mildly abrasive texture, stimulate and smooth skin texture. Leave on for about 10 minutes before washing off. This is more suitable for oily skin; if your skin is dry, add a little olive oil to the mixture. Also a useful mixture to improve skin showing a flaky, faded tan.

Marigold
Used as skin healer, marigold tea made by steeping flower heads — a good handful — in 250ml of boiling water, then straining when cold. This can be used as a mild skin tonic, traditionally helpful with thread veins, or to dab over your skin after a bath. Under its botanical name, calendula, marigold crops up often in soothing hand creams and herbal lotions.

Oatmeal
Oats, under their botanical name of avena sativa, have long

been a favourite herbal choice for treating 'nerves'. More recently, they have been rediscovered as the source of a type of fibre that is particularly beneficial in controlling the level of fat in the blood and possibly high blood-pressure — as well as being a nutritious food. But oatmeal can also be useful externally. It's soothing effects on the skin as well as the nerves have been used as long ago as 2000 BC, when Egyptian and Arab physicians used them. The main ways it is used are in baths, to help dry itchy skin, and as a cleanser which leaves the skin soft and moistened. For bath use you can either add oatmeal to the bath, or rub your skin with a muslin bag filled with oatmeal. For the former, take a handful of oatmeal and add a very little water to achieve a stiff paste. Apply to the skin, and rub with a loofah or bath brush. This is a good cleanser and skin softener. You can also add another handful to the batch water itself. For cleansing, oats are often included in 'scrubs' — fine oatmeal's particles made into a rough-textured paste with honey and a little water are rubbed into the skin of face, neck or back. The oatmeal absorbs dirt, while the rough particles stimulate circulation and dislodge dead skin. When the mixture is washed off, the oil from the oats leaves the skin smooth and soft.

Oat-based non-soap cleansing bars are ideal for washing the face, since they maintain the correct acid-alkali balance (soap is too alkaline), and are non-irritant. They are particularly suitable for acne sufferers, who need to avoid harsh cleansers which will only stimulate the skin to produce more sebum, the secretion that builds up to form acne pustules. If skin problems are aggravated by emotional crises, use oats internally too. Either use oatmeal freely in cooking and porridge, or mince some flowering fresh oats, cover with warm water and after a few hours, strain the extract to mix into a drink with hot water and honey, or juice. Making 'lemon oat water' on the same principle as lemon barley water, using coarse oatmeal, also makes a soothing tea. Homoeopaths use a remedy made from oats, by the name of avena sativa, to treat nervous disorders.

Rosewater
Soothing non-drying toner which you can buy at any chemist. Often mixed with glycerine for first class softener for chapped skin. You can also add some marigold infusion, witch hazel or chamomile tea — all helpful in counteracting swollen or troubled skin.

Vitamin E
Often found in skin creams and lotions, why *is* vitamin E there? Because of its reputation for helping the healing of scars — and by inference, wrinkles. This isn't proven, but many people swear by vitamin E creams, which usually blend the vitamin with oils like wheat germ and almond. Other people like to buy vitamin E capsules, then pierce them with a pin and apply to the skin. In doing so, they are certainly protecting their skin against moisture loss, as the vitamin E is 'carried' in the capsule by an oil such as soya oil, which will 'seal' the skin from water loss by evaporation. Other people claim that vitamin E cannot be of value to the skin when applied externally, and that it is better to take the vitamin in foods such as wheat germ, cold pressed oils and nuts, or in capsules. As no one fully understands how vitamin E works in the body — even though it is accepted as essential for health, it's difficult to judge its usefulness. But it's thought to act as an anti-oxidant, protecting body cells from the adverse effects of oxygen exposure. Until it's understood, applying vitamin E to the skin has to be a matter of trust — but many people are confident that it helps their skin.

Whey
Used in the same ways as yogurt, see page 94.

Witch hazel
Available at any chemist, witch hazel is well known as an anti-bruising agent, and for reducing skin puffiness of any cause. Too astringent to be used 'neat': use it diluted with water, the drier the skin, the more water. For counter-acting puffy eyes or bags under them, soak pads of cottonwool in a mixture of three parts rosewater to one part witch hazel.

Yarrow
Used internally as a 'tonic' and spring cleaner: Infuse about 100g of mixed yarrow, nettles and dandelion leaves in 1 litre boiling water. Leave to cool. Strain, drink a glassful three times a day for a week or so. Cider vinegar and a little honey or lemon juice can be added if wished to add flavour. Yarrow is also used externally — you could use the same 'tea' as for drinking — to treat skins that produce too much sebum, i.e., with a tendency to spots or acne.

Yeast (brewer's)
Well known as a 'wonder food' because of its rich content of B vitamins and other nutrients, yeast can be used as a health-booster for those improving a poor diet. Many people claim it improves their skin on the way. If you take powdered yeast, you need much less than the less strong tablets provide — you need about six to ten tablets a day, unless you find some super-strength ones. Unfortunately, the powdered yeast does not appeal to most people's palates, hence the preference for quickly-swallowed tablets.

Externally, yeast packs are often used for blemished skins.
The yeast tends to bring out latent impurities, so don't
use a mask like this closer than two days before an
important occasion where you want your skin to look at
its best. A typical yeast mask recipe is: Blend equal amounts
of yeast, oatmeal and yogurt or half the amount of olive
oil. Massage into the skin, leave for 15 minutes, rinse off
with cool water.

Yogurt

Use thick yogurt as a useful 'carrier' on which to base your
masks and skin treatments: it will stay thick enough to
smear on easily. It has a mild toning and bleaching effect.
Used alone, yogurt makes a reasonable cleanser, which
restores the natural acidity of the skin, and leaves it soft.
Leave the yogurt on the skin for a few minutes, wash off
with warm water and finish by splashing with cold. Taken
internally, yogurt may help skin by providing a good source
of highly digestible food which the body finds no difficulty
in assimilating, therefore helping it keep in general health.
It can help restore digestion to normal if it has become
upset after taking antibiotics. A yogurt mask for correcting
oily skin: beat 1 egg yolk with the juice of a lemon and
some thick yogurt. This messy mask can be thickened with
oat flakes if necessary, to stay on the skin for 15 minutes;
or be applied on a clean cloth after which you lie flat and
relax until it's time to wash off the mask with warm water.

Index

Uncle Pete

and the

Forest of Lost Things

David C. Flanagan

Illustrated by Will Hughes

LITTLE DOOR BOOKS

Dedicated to my mother, Ena,
and my late father, David.

David C. Flanagan

Huge thanks to the amazing team of Dave, Will and
Gussie for giving life to Uncle Pete and TM's
fantastic adventures

Little Door Books

First published in 2022 in Great Britain
by Little Door Books

www.littledoorbooks.co.uk

Text © 2022 David C. Flanagan

Illustrations © 2022 Will Hughes

A CIP catalogue record for this book is available from the
British Library upon request

ISBN: 978-1-9162054-5-1

Design and layout by Augusta Kirkwood

Printed in Poland by Totem

Contents

Chapter 1

Uncle Pete and TM sat eating their way through the most enormous pile of strawberry jam sandwiches. There was cheese too, lots of it. And homemade chips. They'd also had a plate of beans on toast each as they were really hungry after their adventure to bring the magical blanket back to Harry that allowed him to get to sleep for the very first time in his life.

But to help Harry, and visit Mr Weaver's mountain and tower in the clouds, Uncle Pete and TM had jumped out of their plane after it ran out of stardust.

Later on, as they sailed back across the Night Ocean in Mr Weaver's cloud ship, they'd seen the plane far off in the distance.

Uncle Pete guessed the plane must have been carried along by the great unseen waves of the Night Ocean, but he didn't know where they would take it. Perhaps the plane had crashed and would be lost forever, or just maybe it had landed safely and was waiting for Uncle Pete and TM to find it.

"Are you tired?" Uncle Pete asked TM as they sat on the sofa in his forest cabin with tummies full of food.

"Not really," said TM.

"We've been home for a couple of hours, so it's probably time for another adventure, don't you think?" Uncle Pete asked TM. "We should go and find the plane."

"Totally!" said TM. "Let's go!"

She jumped off the sofa and grabbed the little explorer rucksack Uncle Pete had quickly made for her when they'd got home. He thought she should have her own one, now they were a team and a family.

But then TM scratched her head.

"Where do we start looking for the plane?" she asked Uncle Pete, puzzled.

"I have no idea!" said Uncle Pete. "That's the adventure though. We don't know what will happen, or where we're going, but it'll be exciting and fun. It might even be scary at times, but we should just go and see if we can find it. Otherwise, we'll not know what the adventure will be like."

"Well, ok then!" said TM. "We have to start somewhere though. Any ideas?"

"Yes, I do," said Uncle Pete, jumping up off his seat. "The Forest of Lost Things! It's so big, lots of stuff goes missing in it. I wonder if the plane's in there?"

"The Forest of Lost Things?" said TM. "Have you been there before?"

"No, but I've read about it in this book," said Uncle Pete.

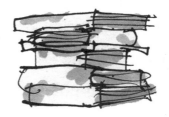

Uncle Pete took a big old book down from a shelf. The book was black and covered in cobwebs. Uncle Pete blew the dust off the front cover of the book, revealing its title which was written in large red capital letters – "PLACES YOU SHOULD NOT VISIT. EVER!"

The book had a whole page about The Forest of Lost Things.

It said all kinds of stuff got lost in it because of the way the winds of the world all gathered there and blew through the forest's tall trees. Giant waves that travelled the world's oceans also passed by the coastline at the edge of the forest, carrying things that got lost at sea.

A compass didn't work in The Forest of Lost Things, so you had no idea of what direction you were travelling. And the trees were so close together, hardly any light reached the forest floor. That made it very dark indeed. So, if you ended up there, you'd definitely get lost and probably never find your way out again. Maybe. But the book didn't really know, because nobody had ever come back from trying to visit The Forest of Lost Things.

"I'll bet we could find our way out of the forest," said TM, who thought it all sounded like an exciting challenge.

Uncle Pete kept reading...

"Listen to this!" he said, reading a bit more from the book. "Legends say The Forest of Lost Things has oak trees that are so tall they reach up into the clouds. They're the tallest oak trees in the world. I just wonder if our plane has got tangled up in the treetops of The

Forest of Lost Things? It's worth a look, don't you think? And it's somewhere I've never explored before!"

TM nodded and asked: "Is it far?"

"I have no idea," replied Uncle Pete. "The book doesn't tell us how to get there. It just says 'Don't go to The Forest of Lost Things. It's a really stupid idea to even THINK about visiting there'. BUT! The squirrels might know how to get there."

Uncle Pete told TM how the squirrels who lived in his forest were a super smart and brave bunch. They'd travelled to lots of places – probably more than Uncle Pete had – mostly looking for stuff to eat, but they were also very curious about the world. They kept notebooks full of information on the places they visited, made maps and were incredibly helpful too.

"If anyone knows how to get to The Forest of Lost Things, it'll be the squirrels," said Uncle Pete. "We'll pack up our rucksacks and make our first stop at their headquarters a few miles away from here. We should bring some nuts – they love nuts – and some fresh notebooks for them too."

And with that, another adventure was under way!

Chapter 2

Shona was the leader of the squirrels. She was very wise and had travelled all over the world, having lots of adventures gathering food for her community and writing travel reports for the Squirrel newspaper, which was called Nutweek.

Shona only had one eye and wore an eyepatch over the other one. When she was younger, she'd lost her eye after taking some nuts that belonged to a particularly grumpy bear. She hadn't realised the nuts were part of the bear's supply for winter and, when he'd found her in his cave helping herself, they'd got into a terrible fight. Shona had escaped, but she now

wore a patch over her missing eye, kind of like a squirrel pirate queen.

Today Shona wasn't fighting bears but sitting at a beautiful wooden desk in her forest office, surrounded by big piles of acorns, walnuts, apricots and other things squirrels like to eat. There was a wooden telephone on her desk, with flashing lights on it, showing there were important calls coming in from all over the squirrel community. She also had a large wooden typewriter for writing her reports on.

The phone on Shona's desk rang, with a kind of wooden sound, like someone playing a xylophone. She picked it up and said: "That's fine. Let them in."

There was then a knock on her office

door. Shona opened it and found Uncle Pete and TM on the other side.

"Pete!" said Shona. "How lovely to see you!"

Uncle Pete greeted Shona and then introduced TM to her.

Shona had a map in her office unlike any other TM had ever seen. It was made from a huge flat piece of polished wood almost covering the entire wall. In the centre of the map was a massive sparkling diamond. Fine lines of silver thread spread out from the diamond in every direction, criss-crossing the wooden map.

TM couldn't read the squirrel words that were written in tiny gold letters all over the map as they were in a language she didn't understand, but each silver line led to a place marked with a precious stone – there were red rubies, green emeralds and blue sapphires dotted all over the map.

Shona could see TM was looking at the map with her mouth wide open in amazement.

"This is our map of our territory showing all of the places we go to get food," Shona explained to TM.

TM was amazed and forgot her manners for a minute. "All of those jewels, silver and gold!" said TM. "You must be very rich squirrels!"

"Rich?" laughed Shona. "No, TM. Those are just pretty stones and metals we find when we're digging around for food.

They look nice on the map, but they're worthless to us. The important thing for us squirrels is having enough food for our families so we can be healthy and go on adventures. That makes us happy."

TM nodded in agreement. She knew just how important families were. And food too.

"What brings you to our community?" Shona asked Uncle Pete and TM.

Uncle Pete told her the whole story about losing the plane and the adventure he was now going on with TM to search The Forest of Lost Things.

"Hmm…" said Shona, sitting back at her desk. "The Forest of Lost Things, you say? You don't want to go there. You'll get lost!"

Shona told Uncle Pete and TM that she knew about The Forest of Lost Things as two squirrels had once gone there in search of a legendary oak tree that had the biggest acorns in the world – enough to feed their whole community for years. But they'd never come back and nobody had heard from them as The Forest of Lost Things probably didn't have a good internet connection, or a post office for sending letters.

But Shona also knew if anyone could find The Forest of Lost Things and get out of it again, it was Uncle Pete. He was a legend in the forest, particularly as he was so kind to all of the creatures that lived there.

Shona said Uncle Pete and TM would have to travel over the sea to reach The Forest of Lost Things. She pushed a button on the wooden phone and another squirrel entered her office.

"Steve," said Shona to the other squirrel. "Take Uncle Pete and TM to the equipment store and give them the stuff they'll need to get to The Forest of Lost Things, please."

Steve nodded. "Please follow me, Uncle Pete."

Uncle Pete and TM said thank you to Shona, who asked that should they reach The Forest of Lost Things, they keep an eye out for her missing squirrel companions.

"Good luck!" she said. "Make sure you come home so you can share your adventure with us all."

"We'll do our best," gulped TM, who was just starting to think that an adventure involving The Forest of Lost Things sounded like a piece of cheese that was, just maybe, a little bit too big to eat.

Chapter 3

Uncle Pete and TM followed Steve the squirrel up a wooden staircase that wound its way up through the forest from Shona's office to a big wooden building built across the branches of the strongest trees.

Steve said the building was the squirrel community's equipment store that contained all of the things they needed for their nut gathering expeditions and adventures. Steve opened the door and asked Uncle Pete and TM to follow him.

There were all kinds of things inside the squirrels' equipment store – lengths of climbing rope, crash helmets, scuba diving equipment – TM was sure she saw a small helicopter made entirely of wood, and what looked like a jetpack, which was also made of wood.

Squirrels bustled around, checking equipment, writing in their notebooks, and trying out new inventions for collecting food (TM guessed that's what the jetpack was for).

"You'll need this," said Steve to Uncle Pete and TM.

Just then, six squirrels appeared beside Uncle Pete and TM holding a large wooden surfboard.

"Take the lift up to Level 8 and wait for the Squirrelcoaster to stop. Get on and ride it all the way to Forest End," said Steve.

"The Squirrelcoaster?" said TM. "What's that?"

Although they worked really hard at gathering food, the squirrels also liked to have fun while they searched for nuts.

So, they'd built a wooden rollercoaster – or Squirrelcoaster, as they called it – that wound its way around the treetops of the forest. It had lots of twists, turns and very steep drops – the squirrels loved those, and they all screamed with delight when the Squirrelcoaster took a big dip and plunged towards the forest floor.

But, unlike any other normal rollercoaster, the squirrels' one had tracks that ran off in different directions, to all the corners of their territory – kind of like a train service, but with a bit more excitement.

When they wanted to travel somewhere in particular, the squirrels would swipe a special wooden card – kind of like the ones that open your hotel room on holiday – into the control panel of the Squirrelcoaster cars. That programmed the car to go where you needed it to. Each little Squirrelcoaster car had a trailer attached to carry equipment and supplies for adventures.

Steve handed Uncle Pete a wooden card with some squirrel words written on it in tiny silver letters. Uncle Pete guessed it was the swipe card for Forest End.

"What do we do when we reach Forest End?" Uncle Pete asked Steve.

"Get off the Squirrelcoaster with the surfboard and walk to where the ocean begins," said Steve. "Get on the surfboard and paddle it out to sea. Then wait."

"Wait?" said TM. "Wait for what?"

"The Wave," said Steve. "Ride it on the surfboard until you see The Forest of Lost Things, then get off and swim to the land. At least, that's what we think you have to do. We don't really know!"

Steve then looked at his tiny wooden watch and checked a tree bark calendar on the equipment room wall. "You'll have to hurry!" he said. "The wave is on its way! Go out that door and up the stairs to the Squirrelcoaster. Good luck!"

Uncle Pete and TM carried the big wooden surfboard through the door, just like Steve had told them to do, and then climbed another staircase. This one was very steep and led to the treetops where they found the Squirrelcoaster waiting on its wooden tracks.

Another group of squirrels appeared and helped Uncle Pete secure the surfboard in a trailer behind their Squirrelcoaster car. Then Uncle Pete squeezed himself into the tiny squirrel sized seat. TM swiped the wooden destination card into the Squirrelcoaster

control panel, which lit up with tiny rubies spelling out a name in squirrel words which she hoped was Forest End.

Uncle Pete and TM's car was right at the back of the Squirrelcoaster and there were ten other cars and trailers in front of theirs, all packed with equipment and excited looking squirrels.

A siren sounded and the Squirrelcoaster lurched forward and began to slowly climb up a very steep track. Uncle Pete gripped the edge of the little wooden car very tightly. TM scurried up his arm and into his pocket, wriggling down and holding onto the material inside.

This was going to be exciting, or a total disaster!

When the Squirrelcoaster reached the top of the climb, Uncle Pete and TM could see out across the tops of all the trees in their forest. It was an amazing view. They could also see the entire Squirrelcoaster track which wound its way up and down, in hundreds of different directions, all the way through the forest. It didn't look terribly safe, but Uncle Pete and TM trusted Shona and the squirrels.

Uncle Pete could just see his cabin from the top of the Squirrelcoaster, far off in the distance. He was about to point out his rusty bean tin shed to TM when the Squirrelcoaster plunged down the first of its steep drops at an incredible speed.

All the squirrels in the cars in front of

Uncle Pete and TM's lifted their little arms up in the air and went "Wheeeeeeeeeeeee!" with delight. It was an exciting ride, but Uncle Pete thought it was probably safer if he held on. He shouted "Wheeeeee!" too.

The Squirrelcoaster turned, twisted and shot up and down the tracks. Every now and again, a little car full of squirrels

and a trailer of their equipment would suddenly head off down a different section of track. Uncle Pete could hear the squirrels still going "Wheeeee!" all the way through the trees.

Eventually, it was just Uncle Pete and TM's car and trailer that were left on this section of track. There were fewer trees here and Uncle Pete was pretty sure he could smell the ocean – one of his favourite smells.

Sure enough, around a bend in the track, they saw the edge of the forest and the vast blue of the ocean stretching off to the horizon. The Squirrelcoaster came to a sudden stop and Uncle Pete guessed this must be Forest End station.

Chapter 3

"Let's go!" said TM, still excited after their Squirrelcoaster journey.

"Yes!" agreed Uncle Pete. "Let's go indeed!"

Chapter 4

Uncle Pete and TM carried the big surfboard down the wooden steps that led from the Squirrelcoaster to the forest below. They walked a little further and found themselves at the end of the forest, looking out across a vast ocean.

The sea was calm and there was no sign of any waves. Uncle Pete and TM put the big surfboard into the water and carefully climbed on board. Uncle Pete lay on his stomach, just like he'd seen in a book about learning to surf and began to paddle using his arms. TM sat on his head, keeping an eye out for the giant wave the squirrels had spoken about. But there was nothing but flat water all around them.

Uncle Pete kept paddling until they were quite far from the shore and then he sat upright on the board for a rest. TM jumped into his pocket and they both

looked around for any signs of the wave. Still nothing.

"I wonder if we've missed the wave?" said TM.

"Hmm," replied Uncle Pete. "I wonder. I certainly can't see any waves. Perhaps we should have a jam sandwich while we wait."

But then TM heard something, far off in the distance. It was a sound like thunder, or an avalanche of snow falling down a big mountain. And it was getting louder.

Uncle Pete and TM looked behind and saw an absolutely enormous wave rolling across the ocean towards them. At one side of the wave, the water was a dark green colour, while at the other end it was all foaming white and roaring.

Trying to remember what he'd read in the book about learning to surf, Uncle Pete lay back down on his tummy, with TM still in his pocket, and started to paddle his arms as much as he could. The roaring got louder and louder and then he felt the wave pick up the surfboard, which began to slide down the green water faster and faster. Uncle Pete was amazed at how quickly they were travelling and he gripped the sides of the big surfboard as tightly as he could.

"Stand up!" shouted TM, over the noise of the thundering ocean. "We have to stand up!"

Standing up was the last thing Uncle Pete wanted to do. He was quite happy lying down, holding onto the board. But TM's encouragement, and the cool pictures he'd seen in the surfing book, made him determined to give it a try.

Slowly, Uncle Pete began to stand up. The surfboard wobbled and he thought it might throw them off into the sea, but he took a deep breath and stood up straight.

"That's it!" shouted TM, encouraging Uncle Pete to stand.

And then Uncle Pete was surfing! With a big grin on his face and the wind flapping his explorer hat, he let out a big whoop of joy! TM was loving it too, shouting "Woooohoooo!" and feeling the salty air in her whiskers.

The surfboard sped across the giant

wave, just keeping in front of the roaring white-water. The water beneath the surfboard was a beautiful greeny blue and Uncle Pete and TM felt as if they were riding a magic carpet. They rode the wave for what felt like years, never wanting it to stop.

A dolphin suddenly popped up in the wave alongside Uncle Pete and TM. It was surfing too.

"Where are you headed?" chattered the dolphin.

"The Forest of Lost Things," replied Uncle Pete.

"Oh dear! You do not want to go there," said the dolphin, before diving down under the wave.

"Look!" shouted TM above the roaring of the wave. "I can see trees. Lots of trees!"

Sure enough, off in the distance was a dark green coastline. As they got closer, Uncle Pete and TM could make out a land covered with incredibly tall trees. They reached far into the sky and clouds covered some of their tops.

"That must be The Forest of Lost Things!" shouted Uncle Pete. "We're going to have to jump off and swim for land as this wave's not stopping!"

"Um, ok!" shouted TM, who was just a little bit worried as the forest still looked quite far away. "Let's go!"

Chapter 5

"Ok, jump!" yelled Uncle Pete. But Uncle Pete had forgotten about all the tins of beans in his rucksack! They were pretty heavy and as soon as he jumped into the water, he sank like a rock.

Quick as a flash, Uncle Pete grabbed TM from his pocket and pushed her upwards towards the surface of the water.

TM swam hard and popped out above the waves, taking a deep breath. Luckily, her little rucksack just contained tiny pieces of cheese and her sunglasses and it didn't weigh much.

She took another breath and dived down to try and help Uncle Pete, but there was no sign of him – he was sinking so fast into the dark, deep water.

TM was sad and scared, but she wasn't about to give up trying to save Uncle Pete. She swam back up, took another big breath and dived again, deeper this time,

trying to see if there was any sign of Uncle Pete. But there was just blackness.

Further down in the depths of the sea, Uncle Pete was holding his breath and calmly trying to take his rucksack off. As an explorer he knew it wasn't a good idea to panic when you fell into water because it made you tired. But his rucksack straps were very tight and he was still sinking.

Uncle Pete's breath had almost run out and it was getting very dark now under the sea as he sank deeper and deeper. But although he was in a great deal of danger, Uncle Pete stayed calm and kept thinking, thinking and thinking, trying to come up with a way of getting himself out of trouble.

Finally, he managed to get his heavy rucksack off his back and was just about to let it go so he could try and swim back to the surface when he suddenly remembered about his new emergency underpants! Uncle Pete had invented them before his last adventure but hadn't tried them out as they needed some extra testing to make sure they were safe to use. He'd packed the emergency underpants into his rucksack for this adventure, just in case he got the chance to try them out.

Uncle Pete stayed calm, opening his rucksack and feeling around inside for the emergency underpants. It was very dark this deep underwater but he found the pants and pulled them on over his trousers – kind of like an underwater Superman. He then let go of his rucksack which sank like a heavy stone down into the depths of the ocean.

The emergency underpants were bright orange and had a piece of string attached to them with a big warning label on it that said DANGER – ONLY PULL IF YOU'RE REALLY IN TROUBLE.

"Here goes," thought Uncle Pete. He pulled hard on the piece of string, just as he was finally running out of air.

Nothing happened for a second or two, but then some little bubbles came out of the bottom part of the underpants – just like when you fart in the bath.

Uncle Pete watched the bubbles drift up past his face and thought the pants must be broken…

and then… WHOOOOOOSH! The underpants inflated instantly, like a lifejacket, sending Uncle Pete back up towards the surface of the ocean at a terrific speed.

Uncle Pete could see the sunlight coming down through the water and knew he was going to be safe. He hoped TM was ok and would see the bubbles coming out from his underpants as he rose faster and faster. He really needed to breathe now too.

TM did see the bubbles as she swam around in circles on the surface and knew it was Uncle Pete!

But the underpants kept on inflating until they were as big as a sofa and, just as Uncle Pete's head popped out of the water allowing him to take a big breath, there was a huge BANG!

The pants exploded and air gushed out of them with a sound like a jet engine, sending Uncle Pete soaring into the sky towards The Forest of Lost Things.

He had just enough time to shout to TM as he shot past her.

"Swim to the forest," he yelled. "I'll meet you theeeeeeeeere!

And then he was just a speck in the sky.

TM was relieved to see Uncle Pete, even if he was now disappearing off into the distance in a pair of very noisy underpants.

She bravely started to swim – not too fast, as it was still quite a long way to the forest and she needed to keep some energy.

TM swam and swam and swam and, after a few hours, she crawled onto a little beach at the edge of the forest, took off her soggy rucksack and fell asleep on the sand…

Chapter 6

TM woke up hours later. She was cold, damp and exhausted, but was still amazed at the sight before her. The trees of The Forest of Lost Things were really enormous. They had big, thick trunks and stretched far into the sky. She'd never seen trees that tall. It also looked pretty dark inside the forest, and just a little bit scary.

But TM knew she had to find Uncle Pete and, hopefully, the missing plane.

The things inside her rucksack were all wet, so she laid them out on a rock so they'd dry a little bit in the sun. It didn't look as if there was much light in the forest, so she wanted to make the most of the sun's warmth now. TM had wrapped some cheese in a piece of brown paper, which was all damp, but the cheese tasted just fine.

Once TM had eaten some cheese, feeling her energy beginning to return, she set off into the trees, heading in what she thought was the same direction as Uncle Pete had flown with his emergency underpants. But she couldn't be sure.

Within minutes of entering the forest, TM lost all sense of the direction she was travelling in.

TM went back the way she thought she'd come, looking for the sea, but there were just trees stretching off all around her. TM's heart beat a little faster, but she tightened the straps on her rucksack and marched off to find Uncle Pete, determined not to be scared.

There were no paths through the trees and, strangely, no animals or birds that TM could see or hear. It was silent, apart from the breeze blowing through the branches.

Every now and then, TM would come across something that had been lost, lying amongst the leaves and sticks on the forest floor, or stuck in the branches of the trees. She passed enormous treasure chests full of jewels, gold and silver, their contents spilled out along the ground like they'd fallen out of the sky. There were things she thought must be thousands of years old and important stuff nobody could find anymore so they'd just written about it in ancient legends instead.

TM saw an old, wrecked pirate ship stuck halfway up a tree and what looked like an alien flying saucer half buried in the ground, but she kept on walking.

She passed lots of everyday things too – lost kites, trampolines that had blown out of people's gardens on stormy days, balls that dogs had lost at the beach, teddy bears little children had dropped in supermarkets and thousands and thousands of keys. It was a strange and mysterious mix of lost stuff.

TM didn't really pay much attention to the lost things – she just wanted to find Uncle Pete and, hopefully, the missing plane. She kept walking, thinking about all the cheese she'd eat if she ever got home.

Meanwhile, far above the forest, Uncle Pete's underpants were running out of air and flapping in the wind.

"Uh, oh!" said Uncle Pete as he slowed down and started to fall towards the trees…

Chapter 7

As he kept falling, Uncle Pete tried to remember if he was wearing any more experimental emergency equipment – a parachute vest, or rocket socks, perhaps, but he wasn't. Instead, he curled up into a tight ball to protect himself and hoped he'd get a kind of soft landing when he hit all the branches on the trees. He shut his eyes and took a deep breath as the treetops got closer and closer...

Uncle Pete crashed through the thin branches of the treetops, which was a bit sore, but it slowed his fall a little. He kept falling though, hitting bigger and bigger branches on the way down, shouting "Ouch!" every time he collided with one.

But then he hit something soft and springy and bounced up again – it was a lost trampoline that had been blown out of someone's garden, thousands of miles away, and gotten stuck in the tree branches in The Forest of Lost Things!

"That was lucky!" shouted Uncle Pete in surprise, but then he hit more branches after bouncing back up through the trees, saying "Ouch!" a few more times. Finally, he landed on a big, wide branch that was pretty high up on one of the tallest trees in the forest.

The tree was tall enough to get some sunlight, so after rubbing his sore bits, Uncle Pete emptied all of the things out of his explorer jacket and spread them on the branch to dry out.

His jacket had lots of pockets and Uncle Pete always kept some emergency supplies. He had a compass, a little knife, some strong string, a small pair of binoculars, packets of honey flavoured cough sweets and a few extra strawberry jam sandwiches. The sandwiches were soggy, but tasted great after his slightly scary surfing, swimming and exploding pants adventure.

While he was up in the branches of the tree, drying his things off and trying to get an idea of where to start looking for TM, he got chatting to an owl who complained about all of the stuff that kept on getting lost in the forest.

"A long time ago, the forest was an enchanted, peaceful place," said the owl. "The winds and seas that swirled above and around the forest, along with a little bit of magic, meant things that were lost sometimes ended up here, but it was all mysterious, special stuff, and ancient items from legends. The forest's magic meant it knew when to hide things that were too powerful or dangerous for people to own because they'd all just argue about it and fight."

The owl looked sad and told Uncle Pete that a few years ago the weather of the world had started to change, with different winds and storms bringing all kinds of everyday things and rubbish to the forest. Now it seemed as if everything people lost ended up here and there was too much stuff caught in the tree branches or lying around the forest floor. The forest's magic had faded, too, over the years.

"And then there's the giant cats," said the owl, sighing.

"The giant cats?" said Uncle Pete, who was very interested to hear about such a thing as he liked cats a lot. "Tell me more!"

Chapter 8

"I'm not scared of you!" shouted TM at the enormous cats surrounding her. But inside, she was feeling really scared and the cats knew it. They could see her trembling slightly as she stood looking up at them, even though she was trying to appear brave.

These were pretty scary cats though, even if you normally like cats. If you can imagine an elephant wearing a cat costume to a Halloween party, then that's how big these cats were. You'd definitely not want one of them curled up on your knee, or scratching your sofa.

And they certainly weren't in the mood for any kind of party now they'd been disturbed by a tiny, shouty mouse.

There were 12 of them, all different colours – ginger, white and ginger, black and white, black, grey and beige. There were some tabby ones with stripes too. The cats had formed a circle around TM and sat, tails flicking, looking down at her, waiting to see what she would do next.

TM hadn't noticed the cats at first because she was so exhausted, hungry and thirsty. She'd been walking through this enormous forest for what felt like weeks and weeks, with no idea of what direction she was travelling.

When TM had finally emerged from the trees into a clearing in the forest, she was almost asleep and shuffling along with her head down, not seeing the cats sunning themselves on some flat rocks.

She'd woken up pretty quickly when she bumped into a huge cat paw, with giant claws poking through thick ginger fur. Her eyes suddenly wide and her heart hammering away, TM had tried to sneak backwards into the forest, but the cats had spotted her as she trudged out of the trees and quietly surrounded her.

TM was now trying very hard not to make any sudden moves. She was also determined not to think about the sad and scary time she'd lost her family to a normal sized cat.

She'd managed to escape back then and had ended up finding a new home with Uncle Pete. But now she was on her own again, surrounded by giant cats in a forest with no end…

One of the giant cats started cleaning its bum, just like your pet cat does, but another – the biggest of them all – hissed "Tiddles! This is not the time for that! We have…a guest."

Tiddles looked embarrassed, stopped cleaning himself and tried to look fierce again.

"You can talk?" shouted TM to the biggest cat – a huge white and ginger one which she thought must be the leader.

"Of course I can talk," growled the cat. "We all can. We're The Cats of The Forest of Lost Things. But we've never seen a talking mouse before."

"You're all lost too?" replied TM, suddenly wondering if she had something in common with these giant moggies.

"Yes," growled the cat. "Each of our owners thought we were too fussy as we kept changing our minds about the kind of food we liked. Can you BELIEVE that?"

TM shook her head. She knew cats were pretty fussy eaters, but didn't want to say anything.

"Anyway, our owners threw us out and, in time, we all found our way to this forest," the cat continued. "It's really enormous and impossible to get out of here, as you've discovered, so it's our home now. We had to eat most of the small animals and birds that lived here, and then moved on to eating bigger things, which is why we've all grown so much."

The cat leaned forward and put his massive pink nose right in TM's face. His incredibly long whiskers twitched a little and then he asked: "Are you alone, mouse?"

TM gulped, but tried not to look worried. Would she be the next snack on the forest menu for these enormous cats? Would she ever see Uncle Pete again?...

Chapter 9

Back up in the tall tree, the owl was telling Uncle Pete about the giant cats who were scaring all of the forest creatures, with no idea that TM had walked right into them at that very moment. The owl said that most of the animals had moved to a distant part of the forest to keep out of the cats' way as they were incredibly grumpy and acted fierce all of the time. "How did they get so big?" Uncle Pete asked the owl.

"I don't know," said the owl. "They were normal sized cats when they first arrived. It must have been something they ate. The forest is full of unique plants and who knows what would happen if cats ate them."

The owl told Uncle Pete that the cats scratched their claws on the trees, bringing them crashing down. They now lived in the bit of the forest that was clear of trees and it was getting bigger as they kept on scratching. The owl waved a wing towards a part of the forest where there were very few trees. Uncle Pete grabbed his little binoculars and, looking through them, he caught a glimpse of what looked like giant cat ears and tails moving around.

"Well, I'll need to sort that out, once I've found TM," said Uncle Pete. "And then I need to go THERE!"

Uncle Pete pointed out across the forest to a tree, way off in the distance, that soared far above the other trees. Its top was hidden in cloud, it was so tall.

"I bet that tree is incredibly old," said Uncle Pete to the owl. "Does it have an ancient and special name?"

"Not really," replied the owl. "We just call it 'The Very Old Tree That's Much Taller Than the Others'. Which it is."

Uncle Pete reckoned that sounded just fine as a name – after all, it was a good description and the animals in the forest didn't really bother with fancy names for the natural things that surrounded them.

He collected his things, said thank you and good day to the owl, and began to climb down the tree to the forest to begin his search for TM and the plane. He was also wondering why there were giant cats in the forest, which didn't sound right at all, but he'd sort that out later.

Chapter 10

Her heart beating very fast, TM slowly pulled off her rucksack and gently dropped it on the ground, watching all of the cats carefully. She thought she might have to move quickly and didn't want the heavy weight of the rucksack holding her back.

"Come on then!" shouted TM at the cat leader. "Try and eat me!" She used all of her fear to make herself seem much bigger, puffing out her chest and dancing around like a boxer.

The cats all looked at each other and burst out laughing, amused at this tiny little mouse challenging them to a fight.

"You're far too small to eat," said the cat. "But we might just keep you around to amuse us. It gets pretty boring in this forest." He then leaned in close to TM's face again. "Or perhaps we'll use you to lure and trap something bigger for us to eat."

At that very moment there was a POINNGG sound from far off in the distance, like a giant rubber band being pinged. TM and the cats all looked in the direction of the sound.

A few seconds later, a giant ball of socks, about the size of a car, came flying through the air. It bounced into the middle of the circle of cats, who all watched it with wide eyes, their whiskers twitching and tails standing on end. The enormous sock ball then bounced again, soaring over the cats' heads and crashing off into the trees.

Instantly, the cats all darted off after the ball of socks leaving TM alone. She let out an enormous sigh of relief, and then heard a familiar voice.

"TM! Over here!"

It was Uncle Pete. He ran out of the trees with a big smile on his face, the remains of his tattered emergency underpants flapping in the wind.

TM ran up onto Uncle Pete's shoulder, relieved to have found her friend.

"Uncle Pete!" shouted TM. "I'm so happy to see you!"

"I'm so happy to see you too!" said Uncle Pete. He explained how, after climbing down from the owl's tree, he'd set out to find TM but, along the way, he'd discovered hundreds and hundreds of lost socks. He thought this must be where they came when your washing machine ate them, or they blew off the clothesline in your garden.

Uncle Pete had been tidying up all the lost socks, thinking he could take them home and give them to animals with cold feet, when he'd heard what sounded like a giant talking cat a bit further on in the forest.

"I sneaked closer and saw the giant cat talking to you," said Uncle Pete. "I went back into the forest and quickly built a big catapult out of fallen tree branches and some rubber bands I found lying around.

I rolled all the lost socks into a ball and launched it at the cats as I knew they'd like to chase it."

"Brilliant plan!" said TM. "Have you found the plane?"

"Not yet," said Uncle Pete. "We have a much bigger problem though."

Uncle Pete told TM what the owl had said about all the stuff cluttering up the forest.

"We have to do something, TM. We have to tidy as much of it up as possible and get it out of here to recycle it. And we need to do something about those cats too."

"But how will we get all the stuff out of the forest?" asked TM. "We're lost and we haven't got the plane either!"

Chapter 10

"Don't worry!" said Uncle Pete, passing TM a piece of soggy jam sandwich from his pocket. "We'll figure it out. But first, let's get to work!"

Chapter 11

For the next few days, TM and Uncle Pete wandered the forest, gathering all the lost things they could find – trampolines, kites, dog balls, teddy bears, keys and more socks. There were thousands of plastic bottles too. They piled all the stuff up in the bit of the forest with no trees, hoping the giant cats were still playing with their sock ball somewhere else. Uncle Pete and TM were just pulling another kite out of a tree when they noticed a very small polar bear with a little rucksack, sitting on a log. The polar bear looked very sad – and a bit lost too.

"Hello there," said Uncle Pete to the polar bear. "You look lost, just like us. You must be a long way from home."

The little polar bear nodded and his eyes filled up with tears. He said his name was Berg and he'd been lost in the forest for weeks. He said he'd travelled to the forest on a big piece of ice, riding a wave just like Uncle Pete and TM had done.

"You came here on purpose too?" asked TM. "We're trying to find our plane. What are you trying to find, Berg?"

"My gran is very old and she can't remember anything now," said Berg, sadly. "She's forgotten all kinds of things and doesn't know who I am anymore. I want to find her memories."

Berg said his gran had been one of the wisest polar bears ever when she was younger. All the other polar bears used to ask her advice. She was fearless and had protected her cubs and grand cubs from big grumpy polar bears and hunters for years and years. But now she was tired and slept a lot of the time. She didn't remember where she lived either and the other bears would often find her wandering in the snow, unable to find her way home.

"Some of the older bears said her memories were now lost forever," said Berg. "I asked them where the memories might have gone. One of the bears said he'd once met a squirrel with an eye patch who paddled past our village in a little wooden canoe. The squirrel had spoken about a forest where lost things ended up, and a giant wave that could take you there, so I thought I'd try and find it."

Berg said he'd packed a rucksack with enough fish to last a week and then he set off to find the forest. He hadn't told his family where he was going. He'd travelled to the very edge of the ice when the bit he was standing on broke off and drifted out to the sea. He'd then been carried far into the open ocean before the giant wave had suddenly appeared. After spotting the forest, Berg had jumped off and swum to The Forest of Lost Things and been stuck there ever since.

Uncle Pete took off his hat, scratched his head and sat down on the log beside Berg.

"That's very sad about your gran, Berg," he said kindly. "That sometimes happens with people, too, when they get old. They forget lots of things and it's quite upsetting for their family and friends. When my mum got very old, she forgot who I was and that made me sad. But, when people – or polar bears – can't remember things anymore, it's our job to do the remembering for them. We must hold onto the happy memories of the time we've spent with them and that way, the bear, or person, continues to live with us in our hearts."

Berg nodded and said he understood. He talked to Uncle Pete and TM for a while about the happy times he'd spent with his gran. Berg was very small for a polar bear, but his gran had taught him to like who he was and not feel there were things he couldn't do because of his size.

"That's like me!" said TM. "I'm tiny, but it doesn't matter. I think big."

"You can join us on our adventure, if you like," said Uncle Pete to Berg. "If we find our plane, we'll give you a lift back to your family. We've also got to get some giant cats new homes, collect all of the lost stuff that's cluttering up the forest, get it out of here and recycle it."

Berg cheered up and said he would help as it sounded like the kind of adventure his gran would have gone on when she was young.

Uncle Pete added: "And, if we can't find our plane, I guess we'll have to come up with some other way of getting us all home. It'll be fine!"

Chapter 12

Once they'd all collected loads of lost stuff, the three friends set off to try and reach the very tall tree Uncle Pete had spotted when talking to the owl. He thought that would be the best place to try and find the plane but wasn't really sure. It was worth a try though.

Uncle Pete, TM and Berg wandered

through the forest for a while, not really knowing where they were going, but suddenly the friendly owl appeared above them. It swooped down and led Uncle Pete, TM and Berg right to the bottom of the giant tree.

"Thanks for clearing up all that lost stuff!" hooted the owl as it flew off. "I hope you find your plane!"

The Very Old Tree That's Much Taller Than the Others was a spectacular sight. Its trunk was enormously wide and it stretched off far, far above the rest of the trees in the forest. The three friends were so amazed by its size and beauty, they all said "Wow!" and stood looking at it with their mouths open.

"We should camp here for the night and, in the morning, we'll climb the tree," said Uncle Pete who quickly made a shelter out of some fallen tree branches. He covered the branches with leaves from the forest floor and laid moss inside to make comfy beds for everyone.

As evening fell, the forest began to light up with the twinkle of thousands and thousands of fireflies. TM had an idea when she saw them.

"Do you think the fireflies would help us?" she asked Uncle Pete. "I have a plan!"

"Great!" said Uncle Pete. "Why don't you ask them?"

TM said she didn't speak Firefly, but Uncle Pete encouraged her to try and communicate with the fireflies some other way.

TM scratched her head and thought for a few minutes. "Got it!" she said.

TM grabbed a twig from the forest floor and used it to draw a picture of a big tree in the earth. She drew a plane in the sky and then some tiny fireflies, swirling around at the bottom of the tree. Lastly, she drew a big arrow pointing from the fireflies up to the top of the tree. TM dropped the twig and ran around pretending to be a firefly – even though her bottom didn't glow in the dark.

Pretty soon she caught the attention of the fireflies, who gathered in a little group over her head to see what she was doing.

"Come with me!" said TM, beckoning to the fireflies. She ran back to her drawing on the forest floor and pointed to it. "Can you help?"

The fireflies hovered over the picture for a few seconds, and then darted back off into the trees. TM didn't know if they'd understood what she wanted them to do. She'd just have to wait and see.

It was pretty cosy inside the shelter and, after they'd all had a tasty salad that Uncle Pete made from plants and berries he'd collected – he knew the ones that were safe to eat, which was very important indeed when gathering food in the wild – they all fell asleep until the morning, dreaming of waves, giant trees and little planes.

After a breakfast of berries, nuts and a slightly damp and mouldy jam sandwich that Uncle Pete had found in another jacket pocket, they began their climb up the tree.

TM led the way, scurrying straight up the tree's giant trunk, stopping occasionally to wait for Uncle Pete and Berg, who were hauling themselves up, branch by branch.

The climb up the tree took a very long time indeed.

About halfway up, TM, Uncle Pete and Berg stopped on a huge branch and were able to look out across the vast forest. It stretched off in all directions for miles and miles and miles, but they could just see the ocean, where the giant wave had dropped them, far away in the distance. Uncle Pete tried to remember the direction the sea was in as he thought they might have to try and sail back home, if they didn't find the plane.

But, as he looked out across the endless green carpet of The Forest of Lost Things, he was also secretly worried that they might not ever find the missing plane. Perhaps they'd have to spend the rest of their lives living here, collecting and recycling lost stuff.

"Oh well," he thought to himself. "It's a beautiful place and, if this has to become our home, then that's ok. We'll make the best of it."

Chapter 13

A few hours later, after climbing and climbing and climbing, TM, Uncle Pete and Berg arrived at a particularly wide branch. While Uncle Pete and TM had a rest, Berg walked along to the end of the branch and then noticed something very unusual.

"Come and see this!" Berg shouted to Uncle Pete and TM, pointing to what looked like a wooden door that was set into the trunk of the tree, just out of sight of where the three friends had been climbing. The door had two arrow shapes carved in the wood above it – one pointing up, the other pointing downwards. There was a panel of wooden buttons at the side of the door.

"That looks like a lift!" said Uncle Pete. Not many things surprised him, but he wasn't expecting to see a lift door in the side of a tree.

Just then, the lift door opened and two very hairy squirrels stepped out onto the branch next to the one Uncle Pete, TM and Berg were standing on. The squirrels had fluffy, overgrown red fur that looked as if it needed a good trim. They were both carrying notebooks, which they dropped in shock when they saw Uncle Pete, TM and Berg staring back at them from the nearby branch.

"Hello!" shouted Uncle Pete. "I'm Pete, this is TM and this is Berg! Pleased to meet you! Do you happen to be from Shona the squirrel's community?"

"Yes!" said the squirrels, at the same time. "We've been here for years and years after we got lost exploring The Forest of Lost Things. Have you come to rescue us?"

"Not exactly," said TM. "We're looking for our plane but you can come along too."

"If it's lost here, then you probably won't find it," said one of the squirrels, who introduced himself as Stefan.

"That's true," said the other squirrel, whose name was Sabrina. "We've been lost here for years and we're squirrels!"

"It's called The Forest of Lost Things for a reason," said Stefan, sternly. "We sailed here on an expedition a long time ago, in search of a giant acorn, but our boat was wrecked by a huge wave. We made it to shore and found a really big acorn, but we've never been able to find our way back to the ocean as the forest is so confusing. We think it might be a bit magical."

Sabrina took up the story: "Instead, we decided to study the forest and record all of the plants and types of nuts and berries there are. It passes the time and could be useful information if we ever make it home. We built this lift into the big tree so we can go up and down to make observations and try and record all the stuff we can see."

Uncle Pete thought the squirrel lift was ingenious. He wondered if it went all of the way to the top of the tree.

"Not quite," said Stefan. "The trunk

gets very narrow a little further on up and the higher bits are always covered in cloud. We can't see anything from there, so we've never gone right to the top."

"Hmm," said Uncle Pete, scratching his beard. "I just wonder if the top stretches into the Night Ocean. This is certainly a magical place, so it wouldn't surprise me."

The Night Ocean was one of the few places the squirrels had never heard of. Uncle Pete told them all about the journey he'd made with TM in Mr Weaver's cloud ship, riding the waves of the Night Ocean. He also told them about how they'd lost their plane and their hope it might be stuck in the forest, or still lost and being carried along in the darkness, far above them somewhere. The squirrels wished them luck on their climb, though they weren't sure about the whole Night Ocean thing as it sounded even more mysterious than the forest they were lost in.

Uncle Pete, TM and Berg set off again, climbing up the tree trunk and into the clouds. It got a bit cold and damp. And then it went completely dark.

Sure enough, as Uncle Pete had hoped, the very top of the tree just poked up into the dark expanse of the Night Ocean. He swayed around on the highest branch, peering into the blackness.

TM shouted up: "Can you see the plane?"

"No," said Uncle Pete. "There's nothing. It's just black. There are no stars up there tonight, no moon and no sign of the plane. Even if it was out there, we couldn't see it, it's so dark."

A bit disappointed, the three friends climbed down through the cloud and stopped for a rest and think on a branch. Then, TM saw something far below them, a sight which lifted their spirits. It was a huge swarm of fireflies, their little lights blazing through the dusk. And they were heading up towards the top of the tree.

"Yes!" shouted TM in delight. "I knew they understood!"

The fireflies shot past Uncle Pete, TM and Berg and headed straight through the cloud and into the Night Ocean. Once they arrived at the very top of the tree, they began to fly around and around it, sending their light out into the darkness.

TM climbed back up the tree very quickly to see what they were doing and then came scurrying back down to report.

"They're making a firefly lighthouse!" she shouted in excitement. "That was my plan! If the plane's lost out there in the darkness, perhaps it'll be attracted to the light."

Chapter 14

As it turned out, Uncle Pete's plane wasn't lost anymore. And it was actually being flown by someone he knew – Inky the cat!

A few days before Uncle Pete and TM had begun their climb up the tree, Inky had been out sailing the Night Ocean in a cloud ship, gathering stardust for his friend Mr Weaver. Inky had spotted

Uncle Pete's plane being carried along by the currents.

Inky turned his little cloud ship towards Uncle Pete's plane and, raising an extra shimmering star speckled sail, he'd caught up with it. Once he was alongside the plane, Inky uncoiled a rope he'd made with special sparkly black wool. He tied one end to the cloud ship, made a big loop in the other and threw it over the tail of Uncle Pete's plane. The sparkly black wool rope was very strong indeed and so was Inky. He gripped the rope tightly and pulled hard until Uncle Pete's plane slowed, then stopped.

Inky grabbed a jar of stardust from his bag – he always kept a supply when he was out sailing the Night Ocean because you never knew when you'd need a jar of stardust – and then, balancing like a circus performer, he walked out across the rope on his tiptoes.

Once he'd reached Uncle Pete's plane, he unscrewed the lid from the jar of stardust and poured it into the fuel tank. He carefully untied the rope from the tail and threw it back towards his cloud ship. Finally, he said "Meow" and the cloud ship turned and sailed back towards Mr Weaver's tower on the moon shaped island, far away in the velvety darkness.

Although Inky could do lots of things, he'd never actually flown an old aeroplane before. He wasn't entirely sure if you could fly an aeroplane through the Night Ocean. But there was a first time for everything and he decided to give it a go.

Inky said "Meow" to himself, turned the starter key and the engine spluttered into life.

"Meow!" Inky made sure his glasses were on tightly, pushed the plane's throttle forward and then roared off across the waves of the Night Ocean to take Uncle Pete's plane back to him.

Of course, Inky didn't realise Uncle Pete and TM weren't at home and, instead, were lost and climbing the tallest tree in The Forest of Lost Things, with no idea whether they'd ever get back to their own forest.

Inky settled in for a long journey, enjoying the rush of cold air in his pointy ears as he flew Uncle Pete's plane across the Night Ocean, riding up and down the unseen waves, with a trail of stardust sparkling behind him. He didn't think it would take him long to reach the daylight of the Sky Above the Rest of the World and then it would just be a matter of hours, or days or maybe weeks to reach Uncle Pete's house in the forest.

But then Inky saw something, far off in the distance. It looked like the light from…a lighthouse? Inky knew the Night Ocean pretty well and he didn't think there were any lighthouses out here. He turned Uncle Pete's plane towards the light to investigate and, as he got closer, he saw that it was thousands of fireflies flying around the top of a tree…

Chapter 15

"Listen!" said Uncle Pete. "Is that the sound of…a plane? Yes, I think it is!"

Up above them, in the Night Ocean, Inky flew towards the fireflies and, just as he reached the top of the tree, he quickly tied a sparkly wool rope to the plane's controls. He made a loop on the other end of the rope and threw it over the side.

It caught a branch and, for a few seconds, the plane went round and around the top of the tree. He switched off the engine and the plane stopped, floating gently on the currents of the night ocean.

The fireflies scattered and flew back down through the clouds, their job done.

Uncle Pete, TM and Berg saw them fly past and were just about to start climbing back up the tree, when Inky's head popped out of the clouds above them.

"Meow!" said Inky, surprised.

"Inky!" yelled TM. "It's Inky! Hooray!"

"Meow," said Inky, who pointed a claw back up towards the top of the tree.

"No, we can't go home yet, Inky," said Uncle Pete. "We have to collect all the stuff

Chapter 16

Inky flew the plane above the clearing in the trees where Uncle Pete, TM and Berg had piled up all the lost things and rubbish they'd found. The giant cats were back, too, having grown bored of playing with their enormous sock ball. It lay on the ground beside them as they sunned themselves. They all jumped to their feet when the plane appeared, watching it fly around their clearing, wondering who was brave enough to disturb them.

The cats were shocked to see the little plane, flown by what looked like a cat wearing glasses, coming in to land right where they were sitting. They watched as the plane stopped, stardust floating through the air behind it. Inky jumped out of the pilot's seat and walked straight towards them.

"Well, well, well," said the biggest cat. "What do we have here? A flying cat? I wonder what it tastes like?" The other cats all laughed, menacingly.

"Meow," said Inky, looking at the giant cats over the top of his glasses and folding his arms. "Meow."

"We're sorry!" said the giant cat, whose name turned out to be Mr Fluffy Tail. "We're not going to eat you! In fact, we've not eaten any animals in the forest! We're just lost and scared. We were hungry and ate some very strange plants, then found ourselves this size. And we're sorry about knocking all the trees down!"

The rest of the giant cats all nodded in agreement. Inky held up a paw, said

"Meow" and wandered off into the trees. The giant cats dared not move an inch as they knew Inky wasn't like any other moggy they'd met.

Ten minutes later, Inky reappeared holding a bunch of different plants. The giant cats all watched as Inky carried the plants to the plane where he took a jar of stardust from inside his bag. He then took out a wooden chopping board and a kitchen knife and began to chop up the plants. He reached back inside the bag and took out a little bowl with CAT FOOD written on the side. He put the chopped plants in the bowl, poured some stardust on top of them and mixed it all up with a wooden spoon.

Finally, Inky carried the bowl full of his special cat food mixture over to the giant cats.

"Meow," he said, pointing to the bowl and holding up a single claw.

The giant cats understood. They each dipped a huge claw into the cat food mixture and ate it.

Almost instantly, they all began to shrink and, moments later, they were all normal sized cats again. Inky, who was now much bigger than them, said "Meow" and nodded, satisfied with his work.

Just then, Uncle Pete, TM, Berg arrived with the squirrels, Stefan and Sabrina, having come down the tree using their lift.

"Nice work, Inky!" said Uncle Pete, seeing all the cats were no longer huge and scary.

"Not so big now, are you?" said TM, who was still pretty angry at being scared by the cats.

"We're really sorry," said another of the cats, whose name was Booboo. "We just want to go back to being normal cats in happy homes. Can you help us?"

"Of course!" said TM, suddenly feeling very sorry for the lost cats. "Stick with us and we'll get you home, somehow. We have a plan!"

Chapter 17

Uncle Pete gathered everyone around him and shared their plan to get out of the forest. He listed all of the different things that would happen, writing them on a page out of Stefan's notebook.

* Stage One – Inky flies the plane back to his home and collects as much special wool rope as possible.

* Stage Two – Inky flies the plane with the wool rope back to The Forest of Lost Things.

* Stage Three – Everyone helps make a giant net from the wool and a big wooden hook.

* Stage Four – Everyone puts all of the lost stuff that's been collected into the giant net.

* Stage Five – We all get into the plane, somehow.

* Stage Six – Uncle Pete flies the plane, picks up the giant net full of stuff with the wooden hook and we get it all out of the forest, dropping off Inky, the 12 cats, Berg and the squirrels along the way.

* Stage Seven – Enjoy a celebratory feast of beans on toast, strawberry jam and possibly chips.

"Simple!" said Uncle Pete after he'd finished explaining all of the different stages of the plan.

TM didn't think it sounded terribly simple, but she knew Uncle Pete could do pretty much anything he set his mind to and she trusted him. The cats had never been in a plane before, so they were looking forward to flying for the first time. The squirrels were used to nutty plans and they thought it sounded like a completely brilliant adventure. So did Berg, though

he secretly wondered if the little plane could lift the weight of the lost things in the big net. And he also wondered how they'd all fit inside. But he knew they'd have to try.

Inky just nodded and said "Meow".

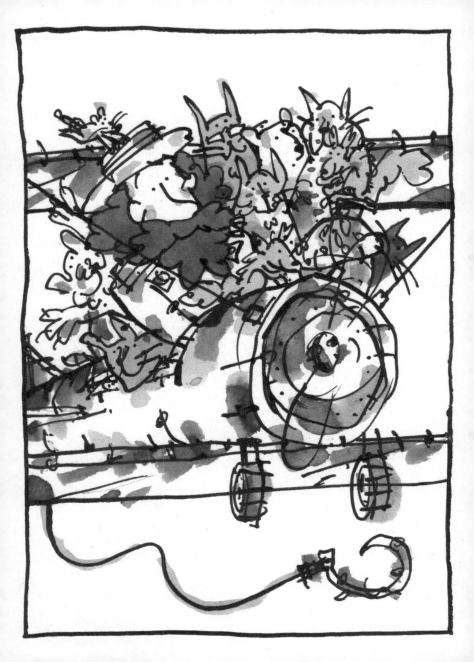

Chapter 18

Days later, the giant wool net was finished, with all of the lost stuff for recycling gathered up inside of it. There was a big loop tied on the top of the net.

The squirrels, meanwhile, had made a giant wooden hook out of bent tree branches, tied together with more of Inky's strong sparkly wool. They attached a length of rope to it and tied it to the tail of the plane. Uncle Pete used some of the lost things they'd collected to make parachutes for everyone, just in case they needed them. The 12 cats chased butterflies and played with spare bits of wool that Inky made into a ball for them.

And then it was time to go.

Uncle Pete, TM, Berg, Inky and the 12 cats all squeezed into the plane. But the squirrels had vanished. Minutes later they re-appeared carrying the biggest acorn any of the group had ever seen.

"Do you think we can fit this in?" Stefan asked Uncle Pete. "It would feed our community for a long time."

"Let's try!" said Uncle Pete, who was

a bit worried about how heavy the little plane was getting with everyone on board. And it still had to lift the big net of lost stuff for recycling.

"Meow," said Inky, opening his bag and taking out ten jars of stardust. He poured the whole lot into the plane's fuel tank and squeezed into the seat beside Uncle Pete,

TM, Berg, the cats and the squirrels, who were sitting with the giant acorn on their laps.

"Here we go!" said Uncle Pete, turning the starter key. The plane's engine gave a load bang and roared into life, stardust spluttering out behind the propellor. "Hold tight!"

The plane was so heavy it took a while to get moving and it bumped and swerved across the rough ground of the forest clearing, its engine straining with the effort, the giant wooden hook bouncing along behind them. Just as everyone thought they were going to crash into the trees, the plane wobbled into the sky above the forest.

Everyone on board cheered, but then they all remembered they still had to try and grab the big net full of lost stuff…

Uncle Pete pointed the plane back down towards the forest clearing where the net lay.

"Hold on, everyone! This could get exciting!"

Pushing the plane's throttle (which is like a car's accelerator) all the way to maximum, Uncle Pete flew as low as he could across the clearing, hoping the big wooden hook would grab the net.

It did. The plane almost stopped dead though, the net was so heavy and even TM thought they'd never get it off the ground, but it was definitely moving. The plane's engine roared louder than ever as it tried to climb up into the air, carrying the huge net of stuff.

But there was absolutely no way they were going to avoid crashing into the trees. The giant net was off the ground, but it was swinging around and pulling the plane back down towards the forest. Uncle Pete gritted his teeth and said "Come on! You can do it!" but the plane was running out of space.

TM looked over the side and saw the tops of the trees getting closer and closer. She closed her eyes, certain they were going to crash when, above the noise of the engine, she heard a hooting sound.

It was the owl! It was flying alongside the plane and TM was sure it was smiling. Why, she didn't know as they were definitely about to crash. Berg was getting scared and thought of his gran and his family back home. The squirrels were shrieking with delight but holding onto their acorn very tightly indeed. The cats were all yowling and screeching loudly, not enjoying their first experience of flying very much at all. Inky was standing up out of his seat, furiously pouring more stardust into the fuel tanks, but it wasn't enough.

"Brace for impact!" shouted Uncle Pete, knowing things were going very wrong.

Suddenly, all the trees ahead of the plane magically parted and leaned over backwards, making a path that led all the way out of the forest and back towards the ocean. The owl smiled again, waved a wing and turned back towards its tree.

"Hooray!" everyone yelled, relieved and happy that they were all on their way, safely.

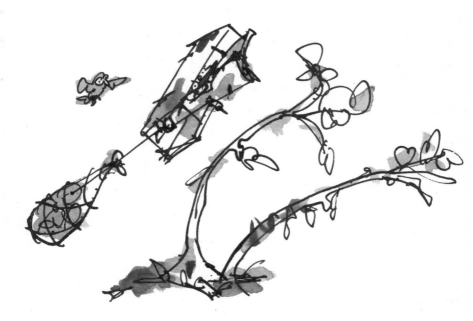

Chapter 19

After all of the excitement on leaving the forest, the journey home went pretty well. The little plane took a while to climb high into the sky, the giant net of stuff trailing behind it.

"Meow," said Inky, pointing to a cloud he'd spotted after a few hours of flying. Uncle Pete turned the plane towards it and, just as they were flying over the cloud, Inky said "Meow" again, jumped out, did a somersault and landed on the cloud. He didn't need a parachute.

As the plane circled around above him, TM saw Inky putting up a sparkly woollen sail on the cloud. He waved and the cloud gently moved off across the sky. Everyone was sad to see him go, but somehow TM knew they'd meet him again.

The cats were next. Uncle Pete flew the plane towards a special place he knew about, not far from where he lived. It looked after cats who'd been chucked out of their homes and found them new places to live, with loving families who didn't mind if they were fussy about their food. Uncle Pete knew they'd be fine there.

He circled above the cat sanctuary, pointed to the cats and shouted: "It's your turn to jump!"

The cats tightened their parachutes, said "Thank you!" and jumped over the side of the plane. Uncle Pete, TM and the squirrels watched all 12 of them float gently to the ground, where they were greeted with bowls of food by the kind people who would look after them until they found new homes.

And then it was the turn of the squirrels.

Uncle Pete had spotted the Squirrelcoaster ahead of them and knew they were back above squirrel territory, so he turned around to tell Sabrina and Stefan when to jump. But they were already flying through the air, still holding onto their giant acorn. They both yelled "Yeeha!" as they fell towards the forest.

At the very last minute, the squirrels pulled the cords on their parachutes and landed in the seats of the Squirrelcoaster.

It shot off through the forest, Sabrina and Stefan still shrieking with excitement and looking forward to bringing their enormous acorn back for a huge homecoming party with Shona.

Although they were now much closer to home, Uncle Pete had decided to drop Berg off last as a trip to the frozen north would be a great way to finish this amazing adventure they'd all been on. Berg was quite happy about that, too, as he was enjoying his time with Uncle Pete, TM and all the others.

So, instead of heading back to Uncle Pete's home in the forest, they turned north and flew for a few more days, Berg peering over the side of the plane as they reached the Arctic lands where he hoped he'd see his family waiting for him.

"I thought there'd be much more snow!" TM shouted to Uncle Pete over the noise of the engine. "And I can't see any polar bears!"

She was right. There was no sign of any polar bears. Berg recognised the place where he'd set off on his journey as the plane circled around in the sky, but instead of his family, there was just an empty, rocky landscape with no snow or ice.

Berg's eyes filled with tears and he suddenly felt very alone.

Uncle Pete turned around and saw how worried Berg looked.

"Berg. The snow's melted so your family must have moved to a colder place. Or perhaps they're out looking for you. Don't worry my little friend. We'll find them together. Come back with us to the forest for some jam sandwiches, beans on toast and some chips. We'll get all of our Arctic exploration equipment together, make a plan and return here soon to find your family. It'll be another adventure!"

Berg cheered up when he heard that and, although he was still worried, he knew Uncle Pete and TM would do everything they could to help him find his family.

Sometime later the three friends arrived back over Uncle Pete's forest.

They couldn't land with the big net full of lost stuff so, above a clearing near his shed, Uncle Pete pulled a lever on the plane's control panel and the net fell away towards the ground. It landed with a thump, but the net held together. Uncle Pete was already thinking about how he would recycle or give away lots of the stuff he'd collected, but that was for another day.

The sun was beginning to set as Uncle Pete landed the plane in the long grass near his cabin. He turned off the engine and let the plane trundle back into the shed.

"Phew!" he said. "That was quite an adventure!"

"That was wild!" said TM, shaking her head. "Are all of our adventures going to be like this?

"Probably," said Uncle Pete, laughing. But then he became more serious. "Our next task is to get Berg back to his family and find out where all the snow has gone. First though, we need to eat something!"

The three friends wearily clambered out of the plane and headed into the cabin. When they reached the door, they noticed Uncle Pete's rucksack lying on the doorstep. It was a bit salty looking, with dried up seaweed all over it. There was a shell stuck to it with a message that said: "Here's your rucksack back. Hope you had a good adventure. Love from Dolph Dolphin."

"Well, isn't that kind?" said Uncle Pete, picking up the rucksack and taking it inside the cabin.

"Beans on toast?" Uncle Pete asked TM and Berg.

"Yes, please!" they both replied. But before Uncle Pete could open three tins of beans, TM and Berg had both fallen fast asleep on the sofa, dreaming of their next adventure to Arctic lands, and their very important search for a missing family of polar bears…

The End

Turn over to discover
Uncle Pete's collection
from
The Forest of
Lost Things

...

Lost Things

(From The Forest of Lost Things)

Can you find all the lost things from Uncle Pete's adventure?

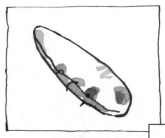

a surfboard

a unique plant

a fancy necklace

the biggest acorns

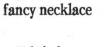

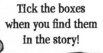

Tick the boxes when you find them in the story!

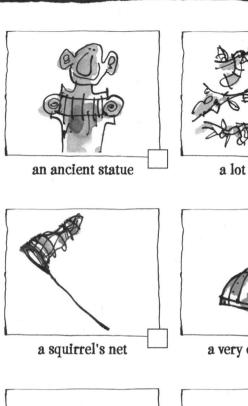

an ancient statue

a lot of socks

a squirrel's net

a very old helmet

a parachute

a giant wooden hook

Thanks for your help young adventurer!
- Uncle Pete